Directions *to* Myself

a memoir

Heidi Julavits

BLOOMSBURY PUBLISHING
LONDON · OXFORD · NEW YORK · NEW DELHI · SYDNEY

BLOOMSBURY PUBLISHING
Bloomsbury Publishing Plc
50 Bedford Square, London, WC1B 3DP, UK
29 Earlsfort Terrace, Dublin 2, Ireland

BLOOMSBURY, BLOOMSBURY PUBLISHING and the Diana logo
are trademarks of Bloomsbury Publishing Plc

First published in 2023 in the United States by Hogarth Press
First published in Great Britain, 2023

A catalogue record for this book is available from the British Library

ISBN: HB: 978-1-4088-8349-5; TPB: 978-1-4088-8350-1;
eBook: 978-1-4088-8347-1; ePDF: 978-1-5266-6311-5

2 4 6 8 10 9 7 5 3 1

Typeset by Newgen KnowledgeWorks Pvt. Ltd., Chennai, India
Printed and bound in Great Britain by CPI Group (UK) Ltd, Croydon CR0 4YY

To find out more about our authors and books visit
www.bloomsbury.com and sign up for our newsletters

AUTHOR'S NOTE

All the people in this book, save my family, are intricate composites. Events have been combined and details, locations, and dates altered to protect people's identities. This book relies on memory. As a result, much of what is portrayed, beyond the intentional alterations, may involve the unintentional creative license that memory can inspire.

Also, much gratitude is owed to the authors of *A Cruising Guide to the New England Coast*, a book I read many times when I was younger, and, through repeated exposure, committed parts to memory, or so I'd thought, until I checked them against the published text. The italicized quotes from *A Cruising Guide to the New England Coast* (1934 and 1972 editions) are slightly edited or collaged to accurately represent the impact these books had on me, and to signal the authors' unwitting collaboration with this one reader. The regular act of misremembering is partly why these sentences were never forgotten.

Finally, this book would never have been finished without Parisa Ebrahimi, my true guide.

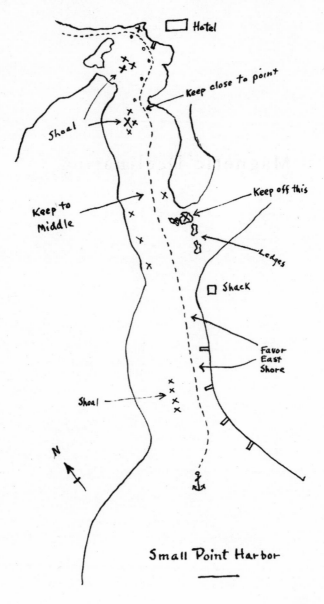

Hotel

Keep close to point

Shoal

Keep to Middle

Keep off this

Ledges

Shack

Favor East Shore

Shoal

N

Small Point Harbor

1937

Magnetic Declination

Here, the road hugs the ocean. The water comes and goes from view because the coast is shaped like a hand with hundreds of fingers, the road tracing the edge of the palm. When visible, the shore is a pile of seaweed-covered rocks, the water between 30 and 58 degrees and some shade of metal no matter the month. The ocean floor is covered with barnacles, mussel shells, and the spiky domes of dead anemones. Water shoes or old sneakers are recommended if planning to swim, along with a healthy sense of personal limits. Islands are farther away than they appear.

The sale is in the next town. My son, who is five, sits in the backseat. He's already announced: He's going on this errand against his will and won't be having any fun.

I promise I'll be quick once we arrive, but I need to drive slower than the speed limit because of the frost heaves. They crack through the asphalt each winter. They wreck the shocks on cars already corroded by the salt the snowplows scatter, to keep everyone's tires from sliding. Even so, people in a hurry end up in the woods.

Nature is always warning: Slow down. Time is moving quickly, why must you move so quickly through it?

We find a parking spot near an electrical pole and walk past a person carrying a plastic tricycle and a rusted Weedwacker. Inside the barn, people politely jostle for position to inspect the offerings, displayed on tables and stacked in boxes. Objects on this peninsula travel in a slow orbit through the houses. Most of our possessions once belonged to people up and down the road. I know which house the rice cooker came from, and the raincoat with the broken zipper, and the amateur portraits of Napoleonic-era naval men. Things leave as well as enter. Our former front door is now the front door of a house we pass on the way to the grocery store.

I steer my moody son toward a basket of pendants and bracelets and rings because that's where his happiness is reliably located. I don't even think it counts as a trick to lead him here.

The used books table, where my happiness is located, is half covered in kitchen appliances so old that the tasks they were meant to ease are impossible to even guess. Art hangs on the wall, including a few framed charts of the area and a grid of knots in a shadow box. Each knot is identified by a bronze plaque. The Surgeon's Knot. The Strangle Knot. The Marlinespike Hitch. A friend hurries by with an armful of sheets—you should totally get that! she says, out of breath—but I already own a shadow box with a bronze plaque. I've recently started to envision the yard sale that will be thrown after my death. I need to curate my posthumous image now, so as not to be inaccurately seen as a person obsessed, for example, with shadow boxes.

Today, the majority of the books on the table are last century's self-help bestsellers and the usual selection of nautical and navigation books. These comprise the local canon. Most appear to never have been read, because people tend to want only to find themselves.

I sort through the piles. A few of the books I've bought at previous sales: *Games People Play, Chapman Piloting and Seamanship, Men Who Hate Women and the Women Who Love Them,* and *A Cruising Guide to the New England Coast.*

It doesn't count as doubling up—or, rather, won't compel future strangers, acquiring my belongings for one or two dollars, to get any wrong ideas about me—to buy an earlier edition of *A Cruising Guide,* because mine is from the 1970s, and this one is from the 1930s. At a glance, the spirit and methodology remain unchanged. Both give directions by telling little stories, often a mix of history, bigotry, gossip, hearsay, and lore. The warnings issued are stern and incessant; the outlook, given the *Guide* is written for people on vacation, refreshingly fatalistic.

Eternal vigilance, the *Guide* reminds, *is the price of safety.*

Instead of compass headings, the *Guide* describes how to enter dicey harbors using local landmarks such as "the high brick chimney of the sardine factory" as points of orientation. Some ledges are marked by actual shipwrecks.

The *Guide* also functions as a self-help book, its cautious wisdom transferable to people, lost or not, without plans to ever leave land.

It is no place for a stranger except in daylight and fair weather.

The approach is through a narrow channel where the tide runs hard.

There are a number of attractive anchorages, some of them of no value in a storm.

My son digs through the answering machines and calculators on the electronics table, the once shiny, future-hearkening machines now dusty and sucking up light. In addition to a bracelet and a ring, he chooses a DVD box set of a '90s television show that's available online, plus we own no machine to play the discs. I grab the *Guide,* a bracelet, a cellophane sleeve containing what look like giant ceramic teeth, and a ziplock bag of postcards featuring reproductions of famous Annunciation paintings.

Outside, people are chatty as they exit the barn, burdened with cast-offs reincarnated as a windfall. Someday everything will reenter the economy, and increasingly cause perplexity. What is this palm-size rectangle with the cracked black screen? My son carries the DVDs in front of him like a divining rod pointing toward the shortsighted past. So much change occurs in fifty years, and even five. Wrecks disintegrate. Sardine markets decline and chimneys topple. The directions for entering a harbor may no longer advise keeping the tall pine to starboard, because the tree was struck by lightning, chopped down, used to build a barn like this one.

We drive back along the coast, the Reach to our right. This is how we find our way around the peninsula—over which shoulder is the water? But even that's a conditional rule of thumb. Salt ponds, rivers, and extreme tides spiral and extend in all directions. The Reach—named because of the southwest wind that blows through it during the summer, allowing the old schooners to travel the length without changing the set of their sails—stretches between the mainland and an island so vast it looks like the mainland. At both ends are bays leading to the same ocean. Determining from which direction the tide flows and ebbs requires a rethinking of tides completely. Here, the incoming tide moves clockwise; the outgoing tide moves counter.

In the backseat, my son is talking about squirrels and how many taste buds they have. They grow even more, he says, if you feed them sandwiches. My son and I share many similarities. We both apologize to inanimate objects when we drop or break them. We both worry we'll be abandoned by everyone we love if we stop making cheerful conversation. We are both, given this anxiety, sometimes misunderstood. Recently, a great-uncle told him, *You're just like your mother. You don't listen. You talk too much.*

I'm half-listening to my son because, to our right, the fog is rolling in. This almost never happens. I grew up ninety miles south of here. When I was younger, the fog was an unpredictable but regular guest. It could arrive in June and stay until September. Each year, it was a question: Would there be any summer this summer?

We don't ask this question anymore. Something warmed or cooled. Regardless, the fog rarely appears and so this place has become increasingly unrecognizable for being so easy to see. When people say their memories of childhood become erased the older they get, I think: My childhood memories were of erasure, of summers spent in a blank. My parents, in the late '70s, decided to buy an old wooden sailboat. It was the equivalent of a used camper van that we drove up and down the coast. My family spent April and May getting the boat ready to put in the water. We sanded and varnished the mast, the boom, the coaming, the rails.

Then we would launch the boat and wait for it to fill

up with the Atlantic. The unknown was not if, but how much.

I've since learned, because my neighbor is a boat-builder, that a boat's first days in the water, and its first times under sail, are called sea trials and shakedowns. These are to identify problems so that they can be fixed. But that's not how it worked with our boat, which came with the slightly concerning name (we did not, due to superstition, change it) *Second Chance*. The boat, throughout each summer, sprung new leaks. The engine was always being fixed yet never was. The point, it seemed, for us and for it, was to live with the problems, to atone for whatever mistakes made by the previous owner that necessitated this reprieve, and to be constantly evading conviction for crimes we'd inherited. Every day on the ocean was a stress test of luck, preparedness, and skill.

We named our dinghy, which trailed off the stern, *Last Chance.*

In my final accounting, the danger, wonder, and thrill outweighed the moist discomfort of being stuck inside a fogbank with family members who were rarely more than twenty feet away, and more commonly within seven, for days on end. My brother's math doesn't agree. Recently, I told him that I wanted to acquire one of the sailboats that were abundantly for sale nearby or even free. Every fourth house had one tarped, on blocks, in the yard.

If you do that, he said, your children will hate you.

The house is empty. My husband is at the grocery store. Our daughter is at the neighbor's. Most months of the year, my husband and I are professors, but we're also functional dependents, living in our boss's building, on our boss's land, in an apartment subsidized by our boss. Having failed to fully enter adulthood, home is still defined by me as where I grew up, more or less, and so we bought this house, thus repeating the mistake of my parents, conscripting our children to spend summer vacations in a vessel that fills with water from below, because the basement is hardly different from the well, which is also a shallow, rock-lined hole in the dirt.

I need to send directions to a friend, due to arrive after dinner. Because our house, unlike our boss's apartment, is difficult to find, whenever people visit us, they need guidance. Before phone maps existed, I'd cut and paste the same "take the X to the Y" paragraph into an email. Eventually, I started to curate the directions to suit each person's interests or needs, such that I knew or could guess at them. I spend a ridiculous amount of time writing these directions, I think because the drive is long, and I experience more than a little guilt, or shame, that my friends have decided they want to see me enough to spend so many hours in the car. To return the affection, or to meet it with an equivalent or even excessive display of thoughtfulness, has a neutralizing effect. The directions aren't an entirely generous act. They're also a means of deflection. They map an escape from my feelings, so that what's overwhelming can become manageable again.

I finish the directions and attach a boilerplate caution: *Bear in mind: the roads are not lines here, but loops. "North" can lead south and "South" can lead anywhere. Once a person, trying to leave the state, drove forty-five minutes south and dead-ended at a fishing dock at the far eastern tip of the continent. Never trust common sense on these roads.*

Outside, I find my son empty-handed. He's used the DVDs as Frisbees and launched them beyond the bamboo patch. I give him my rubber boots and order him into the tall stalks to collect them. It hasn't rained in weeks, but we wear boots outdoors to protect our legs from ticks. The bamboo was planted a hundred years ago to hide the trash pit, now an archaeological site providing inconclusive clues to the house's former owners' activities. Once, we found a tiny crucifix inside a rusted bean can. For some reason, I don't want to accept the immediate transition of the DVDs from acquisition to trash, though I should probably be grateful. My son is sparing me a struggle. When, in the future, I find the DVDs in a drawer, untouched for a decade or more, I'll know that I should throw them away, but I won't be able to do it. They're a souvenir of this regular and otherwise forgettable day that will officially, when the drawer is empty, vanish.

While he lurches around the bamboo, I compare the

old *Cruising Guide* with the one I already own. Both formally contend: A place is defined by the stories people tell to help others safely find it. This is how you locate this island or this harbor. This is also how you locate its people. Here is what mattered to them about this place. Here is what, beyond coordinates, marks it on the map of a collective or individual psyche. *[O]ne Louis Wagner, hearing that Smuttynose was deserted except for three women, and believing there was money hidden in the house, rowed out at night, killed two of the women with an ax, and rowed back.*

Both editions of the *Guide* contain descriptions of harbors and islands my family and I visited, yet often, due to fog, never saw. We both were and were not the *Guide's* target audience. We lived year-round in a place that the *Guide* occasionally described as filthy or "unattractive." We knew where we fell on the hierarchy when we vacationed in the middle of people's workplaces. We knew to stay out of the way of the fishermen, and not to be upset when they expressed their fair opinions of us, by creating a heavy wake on their way out of the harbor at 5 AM, jouncing us awake in our berths. We knew not to be offended by the tight-lipped man who owned the yard where we kept our boat in the winter. We knew if we caught a lobster pot on our rudder, to get into the cold water and dive down to free it, because we'd be costing a person hundreds of dollars in lost gear if we cut it with a rigging knife. We knew that falling-down shacks were signs of hard times and not "picturesque."

And so, we often disagreed with the *Guide*. We also saw value where it did not. The *Guide* dismissed our favorite island as a "stunt" anchorage "recommended only for 'gunk holers' who delight in cramped and unpleasant spots." It deemed our favorite harbor decent for picking up "minor supplies" but otherwise a "rather uninteresting harbor once active in the fish business but now nearly dead."

My son returns with the DVDs. Silhouetted by the sun, and with my boots, his stride, his handful of silver holes, he is suddenly the shape of a boy. The light distorts his edges. His limbs lengthen and thicken. His shoulders grow wide.

Then the boy recedes and becomes a small child again. He drops the DVDs on the porch. I wipe them on my pants and snap them back in the case until they can be hurled at the bamboo again, or their reflective surfaces stared into deeply years from now, past my face and toward the voices locked inside the spiral, with no technology to free them.

He remembers, suddenly, the ring he bought at the barn. What happened to it?

I'm pretty certain it's in the car, where I must have also left my phone.

He takes off to do a loop around the house. His legs take confident steps, as though his muscles have condensed since this morning, when he tripped over a rock and landed in a flung-out heap. No longer elasticated and floppy, his movements extend outward and snap back. But then, the very next second, he loses control, and flails his arms, which tangle in his hair.

As he disappears around the corner, I feel keenly the precipice we're on. I'm certain that a child development professional has given these next few years a name, but I know, because I have an older child—my daughter is ten— and I've gone through this before, that these mark the end times of his childhood. The end times span the ages of roughly six, seven, eight, and nine. Much like the tides in the Reach, the motion during these next four years is back and forth. Eventually, whatever force has grounded this oscillation—from my perspective, me—fails to exert any power at all, and the vector shoots unceasingly toward the horizon, and all I can feel, in the space that used to pull and gather, is a slightly queasy hollow.

My phone isn't in the front seat. It's not in the glove box. Perhaps I dropped it in the trunk, and now it's suspended somewhere amid the life preservers, rubber gloves, towels, sweaters, bathing suits, water shoes, bug spray, cotton batting, theatrical makeup, and recycling. Some see the chaos in my car as proof of a disorganized mind, others as proof of a prepared one. A person never knows when she'll need a rope.

My phone isn't in the trunk, either. The ring is in the cup holder. I put it on my finger as I walk back to the house, past the hundreds-feet-high elm, the last of its kind on the peninsula, and often featured in the directions I write for friends. I regularly touch and talk to it. I want it to withstand the increasingly vicious storms, because I love it very much. Also, how will people find me when it's gone?

My son has abandoned my boots by the well and disappeared. It's like he's already outgrown them and run away into adulthood.

I sit on the well and wonder how much water is in it. We're officially in a drought. I dust off my feet and put on my rain boots. While I didn't grieve my daughter's slow leaving any less, I had another child to mask the pain and play with for a few more years. But my son's end times are coinciding with a different phase of my life. Something inside me has reversed, the way a pump can suck water in and then, with the flick of a switch, push it out. Before, I was accumulating experiences; now, on certain days, it feels like all I'm accumulating is the experience of losing the experiences I'd gained.

I walk over the dry grass to pet the elm. A piece of bark breaks off in my hand. I apologize to the boughs above, which reach over the house as though to hug or crush it. *I'm sorry I'm sorry I'm sorry.* Once a tree person came to estimate the elm's remaining life span, and apparently mine, too. He had long hair and piercing eyes. He looked like the type to provide wise yet cautious reassurance. *Nothing can touch you here, as has been amply demonstrated in recent hurricanes.*

He looked at the tree, and then at me.

I think you'll live to see it die, he said.

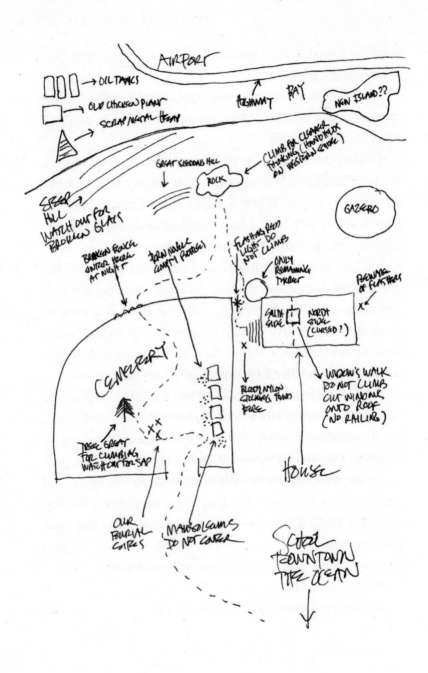

SIX

Here, the trend of the coast turns from north-and-a-little-east to east-and-a-little-north. Fog is more frequent and more lasting and shuts down with little warning. A well-compensated compass, a radar reflector, and large-scale charts are absolute necessities.

My father and I share a fondness for the same kind of hard-to-find pants. When he suggests a road trip to a strip mall forty miles away, it's clear he wants an excuse to show me this place that he and my mother now call home. Sick of the winters, they'd bought an acre of land advertised in a newspaper. A few years later, they gave away almost everything they owned and drove south with a few duffel bags in the trunk of their car. My brother and I jokingly wondered, as we said good-bye, if they'd entered a witness protection program. We weren't sure we'd ever hear from them again.

My father calls the pants store for directions. He says, *yep, yep, got it, thanks.*

The highways are lined with billboards asking questions like "Don't believe in God?" and "Where do we go from here?" A shortcut leads through a town obscured by Spanish moss, after which five traffic circles coil in quick succession. Church signs are replaced by advertisements for the casino located on a nearby ship, because gambling, in this state, is legal only on the water.

The strip mall parking lot is empty. Inside the store, pants are horizontally stacked on a shelf like plates. I want to try pants on. My father knows himself better. He frees a pair from the shelf and walks straight to the register.

We drive back to my parents' new home, the marshes to the left and right like pots of water on a slow simmer, the steam heavy and hovering just above the reeds.

My parents make dinner reservations at a restaurant that overlooks a different marsh. The napkins and the menus are damp and the air-conditioned air is cloying and cold. The food tastes like two kinds of freshness: ocean and cleaning fluid. Our conversational ease ebbs and flows. Sometimes I feel like I'm a journalist interviewing them about their lives; other times, they're the journalists interviewing me about mine.

Tonight, my father asks about the university where I teach, because it's been in the news a lot. A female student accused a male student of raping her, and when the university didn't expel the male student, she vowed to carry her mattress, for an entire year, to class.

Before retirement, my father worked as legal counsel to the state hospital association. He's interested in the university's process for handling allegations between students. By what channels was the accusation lodged? Who sits on the committee that weighs the evidence and makes the ruling?

My mother isn't a lawyer, but she's interested in anything to do with education. For decades she taught high school in a former paper mill town. Years after the factory closed and people lost their jobs, the air retained its yeasty chemical smell.

Unfortunately, I explain, the inner machinery of my workplace has always been a mystery. What interested me, at least more recently, was how long the male student stayed out of the mainstream media. The female student had carried her mattress for an entire semester and received international coverage, some of it laudatory, a lot of it scathing or suspicious, before he finally gave an interview to a journalist.

I'd read this interview upward of twenty times, I say. It felt like a cipher to crack. I'd finally homed in on a single sentence that I'd memorized, because I believed it held a key: *My mother raised me as a feminist, and I'm someone who would like to think of myself as being supportive of equal rights for women.*

I may not understand the inner machinery of my workplace, I say, but I can break down and analyze— some might say overanalyze, to the point of paranoia— a sentence.

Clearly, I say, this man had been taught what he should think but he didn't yet think it. His mother raised him as a feminist, which might imply that his father either was not a feminist or was a feminist but did not raise him to be one, or that, as a feminist in a family of two feminists, he ceded the job of teaching their son to his mother. Unfortunately, her teachings were not enough for him to simply *be* supportive of equal rights for women, itself a legalistic and quaintly '70s way to speak of feminism—no offense implied, I say to my mother, to your ERA involvement—also, in my experience people could quite seamlessly believe in equal rights for women while still demanding that those women have sex with them.

I look at my mother, to doubly ensure she isn't offended by the equal rights mention. She doesn't seem to be. When faced with an ambiguous statement, no matter who's making it, she errs on the side of good intentions. The same is not always true of me.

As a consequence of his mother's teachings, or so her son seems to suggest, I say, since everything he learned about women and how to treat them came from her, he could only state his belief through a double act of disembodiment, by using language that safely detached him from his claims, or rather indicated the degree of distance "he"—the "he" that has a name and is not a generic and conditional "someone"—understood to exist between his actual self and his mother's ideal version of him. Finally, "as being supportive of" was, at best, a noncommittal atmospheric assertion inspiring very little faith that any support might actually occur, or would occur only under perfect circumstances, and would be as unlikely to happen as the sudden appearance, in our solar system, of a brand-new, life-supporting planet.

I drink my sweaty water. I've grown heated and self-conscious. Around my parents I worry that my frequency is too strong, and so I decide to change the subject before their faces turn into mirrors that, when I look into them, I don't like what I see.

To lighten the mood, I say, Remember that foggy summer on the boat when we kept getting lost?

My mother was the navigator in the family—she'd taken courses, including ones in celestial navigation—yet this one summer her talents mysteriously failed her. Each morning, after she laid her tools over the chart, and drew the lines, and did the math, my father would start the engine and follow her compass bearing to the first mark. Except that, again and again, her calculations were off.

We laugh about the mishaps that followed. The harbors never found. The ledges barely missed.

As we're driving home, past the swamp where the alligators live, I wonder why, after deconstructing the sentence where a son accused of assault connects his understanding of women to his mother, that I would want to remember a time when my mother got all of us lost.

My flight leaves at dawn. It's still dark when my parents drive me to the airport, which is bright and peopleless, with only a handful of gates. Nonetheless, they say, their friend once boarded through the wrong one, and ended up in Dallas rather than Detroit.

I line up at the correct gate. I have no connections and nothing to miss.

The apartment is empty, the children are at school, and my homecoming is no longer the cause of anyone's elation. No tiny, undressed children rush the elevator doors to grab my legs. My husband is gone, too, already at work. Though not the case today, it isn't unusual, when I return from a trip, for him to leave. Despite how this might appear, the two of us love each other's company. But we must, for the sake of our careers, alternate absences. Sometimes the connections are tight. Once my husband and I met on the Broadway median with our roller suitcases, the wind from the traffic snapping our coats around and making it impossible to be heard without yelling. Then we kissed, and I took the kids from him, and he took my cab back to the airport.

My class starts in ten minutes. The campus, as usual, is a chaos of crisscrossing human vectors. I stupidly forget that the lawn beside the journalism building is where my son likes to play with his friends. The campus, for them, is an after-school park. Sure enough, he's standing with two other boys under a tree, while their babysitter, a student, reads a book. He and his two friends fling and jerk and yell and laugh.

I consider avoiding him so I'm not late, but I can't, or rather my body can't. I approach from behind and hug him so hard that he'll know: It can only be me. A nearby woman watches with a look of concern. Even since I became a parent, the public interest in me changed, the catcalling switched out for silent, and sometimes not-so-silent, surveillance and evaluation. No longer did I hear *Where'd you get that ass?* My baby became the new focal point of public curiosity and assessment. *Do you think she might be hungry? Don't you think she's cold?*

But then the woman breaks into a smile.

Oh, what a pretty girl! she says.

My son drops to the ground. He's so preoccupied by a problem with his socks that he doesn't register how yet another stranger has mistaken him for a girl. Even as recently as last year, he didn't care when people called him "she." Now that he's six, he cares.

I smile back at the woman as if to say, *Thank you, thank you so much!* I just need her to leave without making the situation worse. Then I crouch next to my son, who's almost in tears. He pulls his socks violently, as though trying to extend them over his head to hide. While nothing obvious seems amiss with the two other boys, it's clear that the problem is not with his socks, but with them.

I put down my backpack and roll up my sleeves, as if to imply, *this is indeed a* very *serious sock problem.* I stretch his socks high and fold them down low. I do this repeatedly while saying, I'm a sock perfectionist! because the other two boys are growing impatient, and I want to make sure I take the blame for postponing their fun.

After a few minutes, my son relaxes; tears no longer push at the periphery of his face.

I hold on to his ankles and ask, How does that feel?

To the boys, who are standing nearby, I'm referring to socks. To my son, I'm offering a confidence boost: *Whatever was happening with your friends, I think you're fine now.*

Usually, he would lift his face for a kiss. This time, he doesn't even answer. He looks at me, and then at his friends, and rolls his eyes.

He wriggles out of my hands and runs away.

After class, my friend and I meet at a café that's perfected the art of low expectations. The fries are tasteless tubes of slightly warmer air unless heavily salted. I unscrew the top to the clogged shaker, and pour salt into my hand, and scatter it liberally, while telling her about the sock incident. These next four years, the end-of-childhood times with my son, I'm starting to suspect, might involve different kinds of grief than they did with my daughter. I'm losing control of something I hadn't quite known I would.

Because, like me, this friend is a catastrophist, I expect her to knit her brows and spin into a globalized doom orbit, and then we can hold hands and stare at each other and scream.

Instead, she says, Didn't your daughter behave the same way at his age?

My daughter mocked me in private, I say, but not until she was older. Also, her disdain was *for me*. It was real. It was *between us*.

My son's disdain, I say, wasn't real and it wasn't between us. It was an act he performed for his friends.

I don't tell her how my strategy to protect him, when he was struggling to connect with his friends, was to redirect the blame for that failure toward myself. Was this why he rolled his eyes?

He's just beginning the process of separation, my friend responds, all smoothness and calm. Her face has no visible working muscles these days. She's been taking a lot of the tinctures her wife sells on the internet.

The waiter appears with a second plate of fries.

She stares across the table compassionately, as though trying to administer reassurance through her extra-large pupils.

Such behavior is natural, she says, starting to eat. She doesn't even bother with the salt.

The car's CD player is broken. Someone fed coins into the slot. There's only one culprit, but it's not fair to point fingers at him. He was often left, when younger, to play in the car. He fiddled with the knobs and put money in the stereo. He would sit in the driver's seat and turn the wheel and go nowhere for hours.

Without any music or audiobooks, my son and daughter have nothing to entertain them on the five-hour drive except me. They request to hear "true" stories about my life, the implication being that I'll tell them untrue stories unless they specify.

My past, unfortunately, has proven to be a finite fossil fuel. I've already plundered and burned all the resources. The only solution is to retell the same stories, but with more detail each time, making them, in theory, truer and truer.

In the rearview mirror, they wait.

I fire up the memory rig and jab the dry ground. They don't yet suspect that these true stories double as propaganda, meant to establish me as an interesting person about whom they'll tell stories in the future. I want to give them the gift of good material over which I might assert some editorial control.

Unfortunately, I was not the kind of child who took adventures or risks or did anything much beyond feel homesick and read. But the house my parents bought in 1972 made up for my shortcomings as a protagonist. The house was a two-family Victorian built in 1888 by a naval man for his two daughters. It had a widow's walk and, at one time, matching turrets. The backyard bordered a decommissioned cemetery that hadn't seen a new dead body since 1852.

Here, in this house, I'd told my children, the naval man's daughters lived side by side on a hill overlooking a bay and a valley. Their father, however, failed to foresee the creep of industry. By the 1970s, a chicken-processing plant had shrunk the bay by a third, and a highway bifurcated the foreground, and an airport paved the valley. The house was surrounded daily by a foul stink, located within earshot of the traffic, and directly under the flight path of the descending planes. After a few near strikes, the airport installed a giant pole at the edge of the house's lawn. At the top was a red warning light that blinked all night and also when the fog was thick. Still, the pilots often flew too close.

My children are growing impatient.

Just tell us a story, my son says.

The rig groans and rattles and discovers a weak, new trickle.

Once, I say, a teenage boy decided to jump the hurricane fence at the bottom of the airplane pole. He used the little metal footholds, meant for the repairmen, to climb to the top of it. Halfway up, he panicked. He clung to the pole and cried for help. Firemen had to rescue him.

The backseat is silent.

I don't like the ending, my son says.

True stories don't have "endings," I say. They have morals. The moral of this story is: This boy learned that he didn't know himself as well as he thought he did.

Their faces are blank. I feel a flicker of panic. If I can't command their respect and attention simply by opening my mouth, I'm not automatically of interest to them, and soon I'll no longer be worth listening to at all.

Fear of irrelevance makes me impulsively say: Do you want to hear a story about an attempted murder?

The minute the offer leaves my mouth, I want to retract it. But there's no backing out. They love true crime stories, especially my son. When asked, recently, what kind of movies he liked, he responded, *inappropriate ones.*

They so desperately want to hear about the almost-murder that they strain against their belts.

I quickly work out the "plot," and what it will and won't contain.

When I was a little girl, I say, my neighborhood was often visited by three types of lonely men. The first type of man sat in the cemetery after dark to drink wine and read pornographic novels. The second type of man hung out with other men in the park gazebo and played music from a portable radio and got into fights and sometimes stabbed people. The third type of man exposed his penis to women while they were out walking, or to girls like me waiting to be picked up from basketball practice.

I check the rearview. Neither of my children is shocked to hear that adult men showed their penises to me when I was young.

While this might make the neighborhood sound scary or dangerous, I say, for me it wasn't. The men understood their places. The flashers kept their distance. The gazebo parties shut down by 1 AM. If the cemetery drunks hadn't left their novels and empty wine bottles under the mausoleum overhangs, no one would have known they'd been there.

So how *did* you know? my daughter asks.

Because, I say, my friends and I played in the cemetery after school. We collected the novels and buried them in a hole. After school, we'd dig them up and read them.

Did Grandma and Grandpa know you did that? she asks.

My impression was that they knew very little about

what I did after school, I say. Nonetheless, I felt incredibly safe and well cared for.

But would you have gotten in trouble if they'd known?

I catch my daughter's eyes. Whenever she asks questions, the immediate answers don't appear to interest her. Predating her ability to speak, she's been working on a long-term project, the present moment representing one of a million data points she's assembling for an undetermined future purpose.

No? I say.

I don't mention how I used to sneak into the back room of the smoke shop where my father bought his bulk cigarettes on Saturday mornings, and where he liked to chat about local matters with the owner and his brother. The back room of the smoke shop was where the pornographic novels were sold. That early in the day, nobody was ever there. Then, as now, I somehow found it bolstering that the cemetery men, rather than skimming magazines, practiced a more literary form of porn consumption.

Did you tell them about the flasher? she asks.

Definitely, I say.

And did they call the police?

People rarely called the police, I say.

She's skeptical. The story is slipping out of my hands. My whole family suddenly seems like that boy who climbed the pole.

Just tell the story, my son says.

Late one night, I continue, when everyone was asleep, my parents heard a scream under their bedroom window. They ran downstairs and opened the back door. There, lying on our porch, was a woman, bleeding from multiple knife wounds.

This time, I say, they *did* call the police. But first they took her inside and gave her water and a blanket.

Where were you? my son asks.

In bed, I say. Your uncle and I slept through the whole thing.

He cocks his head, working out what strikes him as an inconsistency. How loud could the woman have screamed if she didn't wake us up? How almost was this almost-murder?

Then what? my daughter asks.

The police arrived, I say. Finally, the woman was calm enough to talk. She waited tables at a bar near the docks and had just finished the late shift. As she was about to unlock the front door to her apartment building, a man grabbed her and forced her into his car. He drove her to the cemetery, dragged her into the dark corner by the mausoleums, and attacked her with a knife. The entire time, he wore a nylon stocking over his face, so that she'd never be able to identify him.

But she fought back, I say.

Did she know karate? my son asks.

In survival situations, I say, you can discover talents you might not know you had.

I tell them how one policeman took the woman to the hospital while the other searched the cemetery for the man, who was never found.

Grandma and Grandpa went back to bed, I say. In the morning, Grandma took a mop outside to clean the blood off the porch.

I insert a dramatic pause.

That's when she found the nylon stocking, I say. The one the man had worn over his face. It was lying, covered in blood, at the bottom of the porch stairs.

Their mouths drop open.

Either the cops missed it, I say, or the man returned to our house after your grandparents thought it was safe to go back to bed.

The backseat is quiet. I can tell they're impressed. Then I feel awful. A real woman nearly died so that I could enjoy this moment of success with my children. Also, I've violated the "true" terms they demanded. My parents found the nylon stocking immediately after they pulled the woman into the house.

But I wanted to give the story a good ending.

The car needs gas. My daughter takes my son to the restroom, located inside a convenience store. No one can pee without succumbing to the temptation, afterward, to buy a giant lemonade or soda (there are no medium-size drinks), which will necessitate another stop, fairly immediately, at the next rest area, where the bathrooms are also located in the convenience store, and on it goes.

After activating the gas pump, I hand her the credit card.

The pump's numbers flick by. Part of the reason this woman is on my mind: I'd recently texted my mother to find out what really happened that night, because I'd never heard the adult version, I'd only ever heard the child one.

Yet my mother confirmed what I somehow already knew. The man, she'd texted, tried to rape the woman who'd ended up on our back porch, but couldn't because he had "some type of injury." He was later arrested in Louisiana for murdering a woman. His inability to have sex with women (according to the newspapers, or maybe this was just my mother's analysis) made him want to kill them.

This is all probably more than you want to know! she wrote.

A man in a truck pulls up behind me, aggressively close to my bumper. I flash him a friendly smile and ease the pressure on the handle, cutting the flow by half.

As the gas trickles into the tank, I wonder: Is a person protected (or harmed) *from* knowing or *by* knowing? Is the best kind of knowing the kind you figure out on your own, rather than being told? The pornographic novels my friends and I found in the cemetery weren't the first to teach us that there was a story beneath the story, one we had to be alert to and learn to decode. Those novels weren't only about sex; they were about women who found themselves tied up, lacking names, good only for their holes. It was difficult to connect the appeal of these plots to the cemetery men, who seemed so hunched and defeated. At dusk, they'd slip through the break in the hurricane fence with their paper bags, lumpy and filled beyond their limit, requiring the men to cradle them in their arms to keep the bottom from falling out.

The man in the truck glowers through his windshield. My finger still works the nozzle like a trigger I'm never quite pulling. At around the time when my friends and I were burying novels in the cemetery, my parents gave me a book of Greek myths. The Io myth, because of the illustration that accompanied it, remained, decades later, the one I remembered most vividly. Io was the young, mortal girlfriend of Zeus. When the two were caught by Hera, Zeus turned Io into a cow to protect her from his wife's infamous rages. What made logical sense at first made less the more times I read it. The less sense it made, the more it eventually did. Questions became statements as the subtext became the text.

Why was Zeus, a god, always in a relationship with a mortal "girl."

Why was Hera considered so fearsome and powerful, when really her only "power" was to try to murder her husband's illegitimate children or creatively torture his girlfriends by tying them to trees or depriving them of speech.

Why did Zeus's turning Io into a cow amount to his protecting her.

My children return with chips and drinks. My son

doesn't look at me. He's something between humiliated and annoyed.

My daughter interprets.

When he tried to enter the men's room, she says, a man stopped him and said, "The little girl's room is over there."

And what did you say? I ask.

I told him he was a boy, she says, and then he ran away.

The man in the truck honks his horn. I over-mime a sorry that means fuck off. Another man, fresh out of the convenience store, supports a plastic bag in his arms, so distended with heavy items the opacity is threatened and I can almost see inside. He clocks my daughter and visibly tenses. As he passes in front of the car, he shoots me a sheepish glance and tucks the plastic bag deeper into his coat. *Was he the man at the restroom who mistook my son for a girl.* The question is a statement. I know the answer without needing to be told.

The water arrives quickly. Also, the bread. While I wait for my friend, I pretend not to eavesdrop on the only other customers. One is pregnant. The other leans toward the center of the table and drops her voice, as though sharing a secret that only a pregnant person has earned the right to hear:

There's nothing like a boy's love for his mother, she says. It is a gift.

My friend appears. She's wearing a combination of items that belong to people she's never been. She works for an environmental agency and has a daughter whose age is still counted in weeks.

I tell her about the conversation I'd overheard. I

whisper so that the two women can't do to us what I've been doing to them.

When I was pregnant with a son, I say, so many women said this exact same thing to me. I didn't want to disagree with them, because my son wasn't even born yet. Who could say what kind of love for me was inside of me?

I was told, my friend says, when people knew I was having a girl, that she'd steal my beauty.

She sounds oddly excited by this prospect.

But I didn't think it could be possible, I say, that a son could love me more than my daughter did. We loved each other so much that in third grade, she wrote a letter every night and left it under my pillow. I wrote a response and slipped it under her door. The letters are in a box tied with twine. I plan, on some future special day, to open it.

Her love is also a gift, I say.

A waiter arrives to take our order. I want a steak, but out of politeness listen to him talk about a fish farmed in Spain.

This fish is so special, he says, it reshaped the migratory patterns of European birds.

My friend asks the waiter how it could possibly be a good thing, that a fish could disrupt the internal compasses of birds across an entire continent.

Why can't the farmer just raise some fish, she says, and leave the sky alone?

The waiter stumbles toward an explanation and I feel the need to save him. He's just the messenger. He has nothing to do with this fish, save to carry it dead on a plate.

But my point, I say, after the waiter leaves, isn't to convince anyone how lovable my daughter found me to be. I just want to explain why I doubted these women's predictions about a son. I felt vindicated when, as a newborn, he suffered the usual fussiness, but he never once cried when I left the room or even when I handed him over to a stranger.

You gave him to strangers? my friend says. She's not being judgmental. She's just wondering what's possible. She's returning to work soon.

They were strangers to him, I say. But when these women claimed that the love of a son was incomparable to any other love, I started to wonder what they were really saying. Did they mean that the love was absolutely comparable, and the comparison being made was to the love of a daughter? Did these mothers experience, or wish to experience, one love to be stronger than the other, because the loss of intimacy they anticipated as their sons matured promised to be far greater and more unrecoverable?

A daughter's a daughter for the rest of her life, my friend says. A son is a son 'til he takes a wife.

She smirks. Like the rumor that her daughter would siphon off her beauty, this is also silly, old-fashioned bullshit. Still, I sense that she's relieved to have a daughter rather than a son, as if on some level—the one that's visible only when a person has not slept in weeks—she believes this particular old bullshit or worries it might be true.

The avenue is sunny and warm, and unprotected by the wind, which blows from the south, and smells of ocean, rather than river plus land. An older woman and a young man walk toward me holding hands. At first, I mistake them for May-December lovers. But as they get closer, the woman, it's clear, is the young man's mother. I'm so touched by the sight of a son old enough to be mistaken as his mother's lover, still holding his mother's hand in public, I spike an emotional fever. Until this year, I always held my son's hand as we walked along the busy street that leads to his school. But now he can be trusted not to spontaneously drift into traffic. These days my hand is empty.

The school lobby is chaotic. The teenagers expand into every available void, while the younger children navigate the lower altitudes. I'm so, so happy when, once my son and I are outside, he asks to hold my hand. It's cold and he didn't bring mittens. Inside my hand, his is hot and scaly.

At home, I coat his hands in eczema ointment as he complains. I try to distract him by suggesting we look up our hand type, because he and I have the same hands. Seconds after he was born, as the endorphins lifted me above my body, his hands were all I could see, these hands of mine that had come out of me.

Fortunately, I own a book called *Cheiro's Language of the Hand.* When I was around thirty, I started to purchase books I'd loved when I was younger if I ever saw them at barn sales. I didn't think of these books as "for my children"; I wasn't necessarily planning to have any. But the books exerted a guiding pull—both to the past and the future—and the purest way to respond was to buy them.

He lies on the couch with his legs over my lap. I flip between the illustrations of different hand types as we hold ours up and compare. We suffer a collective instant of denial—*maybe our hands aren't* entirely *square*—before accepting the truth.

"These are people without aspirations. They but eat, sleep, and die."

People with square hands—the "lowest type"—are, according to Cheiro, resistless in war and undemonstrative in love. They are stubborn and secretive, violent but not courageous. They possess very little mental capacity, "and what they do possess leans more to the order of the brute."

I grab my son's greasy hands and press them together.

We should start a secret society called the Order of the Brute! I say. As the Order's first item of business, we must make a ritual sacrifice.

His football cards are on the table. He chooses a famed cheater from the pack. We kneel on the kitchen floor around a copper pot. I let him hold the match and hover it over the cheater's face. The table of contents from *Cheiro's Language of the Hand* suffices as a chant.

> *The star on the mount of Jupiter*
> *The star on the mount of Saturn*
> *The star of the fingers*
> *The cross*
> *The square*
> *The island, the circle, the spot*

The cheater smolders and turns green and fails to catch.

My son returns to the living room to watch a show while I wash celery and flatten *Cheiro's Language of the Hand* with a vinegar bottle to read more about "cheiromancy." According to Cheiro, many outcomes are indicated by the lines of the palm. Each page features a drawing of a hand, marked by forking paths. Since my future has already half come to pass, I'm more interested in my son's. He could suffer poor health or enjoy a long life. He could be sensitive and thus too cautious, or he could, through "defect of temperament," rush "blindly into danger or catastrophe." He could undertake voyages, court accident, prove a suicide or a murderer. His hand contained so many possible versions of himself that I can't, as a novice, discern, not even with the help of Cheiro.

"I cannot and will not pretend, as do the generality of writers on this subject, that it is an easy matter."

That night, in his bed, I spread his palms wide and try to read them. But the skin is swollen and raw. Lines are indistinguishable from wounds. If the hand was a map that led to a future person, was there any changing the destination? Or was the destination fixed? A novelist I sometimes cite as an influence once wrote: "I am so afraid that I can only accept that I got lost if I imagine that someone is holding my hand." Because my son's palms are so tender—the lines, if I squeeze too hard, might be vulnerable to permanent and haphazard change—I don't hold his hand as he falls asleep. Instead, he holds my hand in his.

Campus is empty. On warm days, students line the wide steps that lead from the plaza to a pillared, domed building called a library, though no books are kept there. Now it's a giant events space supported, underneath, by administrative offices that dot the disorienting, circular hallway. The staircase is more like a terraced, south-facing hill. Did the university planners, a century ago, take that aspect into account, where growth was concerned? On these steps, the students, like crops, could flourish?

Guarding the steps, or presiding over them, is a statue called Alma Mater. She's not only Our Mother, she's also the university's intellectual mascot. She wears robes and a crown of leaves. She sits in a throne holding a scepter. She's alternately a revered symbol of wisdom and an aloof, institutional collaborator, passively over-seeing, or refusing to see, injustice, corruption, unfair-ness. She's photographed at graduations and reunions. She's the target of protests and vandalism. Once she was given a pedicure. Once the top of her scepter was stolen and abandoned in a restroom. Once she was partially blown up by a bomb.

The café is just east of a gabled brick house, an archi-tectural anomaly on campus. It's the only remaining evidence that a nineteenth-century asylum once occu-pied these same city acres, a history that the university doesn't mention in its promotional materials, or on its tours.

When the former student finally arrives, he's a streamlined assemblage of book bags and stress. He graduated a few years back and is in school again, study-ing law.

In the meantime, he's written a novel and wants ad-vice.

When his phone buzzes, he muffles it under his sweater, which he's removed, because the buildings on campus, no matter the season, are steam-heated to 80-plus degrees.

He and his classmates, he explains, gesturing toward the phone, are analyzing a "found text" for an assign-ment that's due tomorrow. They'd decided to study the letters written by the parents of a young man who'd been convicted of sexually assaulting an unconscious woman. The letters were addressed to the judge and meant to persuade him to give their son a lighter sentence.

I'm curious to know, I say, when you analyzed them, what you saw.

He retrieves his phone and pulls up the father's letter.

The father, he says, uses the word *culture* a lot. He makes excuses and blames everyone and everything except his son. He's basically saying, both intentionally and unintentionally, that men can't be trusted to teach other men how not to hurt women, not even when those men are fathers, and the men they're teaching, their sons.

Then he pulls up the mother's letter. She describes her son as easygoing, kind, considerate, respectful, goal-oriented, hardworking, dedicated, polite, coachable, studious, humble, introverted, shy, gracious, trustworthy.

She's throwing everything at the wall, he says, rolling his eyes. Also, "goal-oriented," "hardworking," and "dedicated" only weaken her case. It can't be a casual thing, to do what he did.

He looks again at the letter.

One of my classmates was an English major in college, he says. She's interested in how the mother's letter shifts between genres. At first, it's an amoral and pretty lame attempt at legal persuasion. Then it devolves into a messy diary entry for whom there's no clear intended audience save herself or the universe or, because she mentions church at one point, God.

He starts to read aloud from the letter. He looks toward the ceiling, as he must imagine the mother, begging for clarity, had looked toward the sky.

"WHY? WHY?"

He receives a text and quickly answers it.

One of the things we've been discussing, the student says, collecting his things, is the possibility for reeducation and rehabilitation.

For parents? I ask.

For anyone, he says. But if you want my opinion, by the time a person's eighteen, it's already too late.

Outside, it's drizzling. I pass the remaining asylum building. When in operation, it was called a "villa" and reserved for wealthy male patients. Now it's the home of architectural preservation and romance language philology.

Everyone's hurrying to class except a cluster of tourists in deli rain ponchos, taking photos beside Alma Mater. Today, she looks like a grave marker. Someone has left flowers on her plinth. My rain boots make a persistent, one-syllable noise as I suction across the wet pavers. *Why? Why?* Maybe the mother, in her letter, wasn't addressing the judge, or herself, or the universe, or God. Maybe she was addressing her son. Why had he done it? Why had he become this man?

The weather outside has been gray and cold for over a week. The weather inside our apartment is the same. When everyone is asleep, I go online and find a cheap, hundred-year-old resort in the nearby mountains. Based on the photos, the hotel will be staffed by people dressed like nurses, have spotty heat, serve bad coffee, and offer period eccentricities, like an umbrella stand full of walking sticks, that only I will enjoy.

The next morning, everyone holds their breath as the car slips through a tunnel and exits into the middle of a colorless mountain range. Pretzel factories and vinyl-clad houses line the road. Nobody in the backseat asks for a story, true or not.

Since my husband is driving, and I'm the one holding

the phone, it seems like a natural segue to tell my children about their grandmother, and how she was a very skilled navigator.

She was so skilled, in fact, I say, she didn't need electronics to chart a course. She'd even learned an ancient practice called celestial navigation.

Neither of them asks what celestial navigation is.

On clear nights, I say, using the North Star as a guide, a person can, after calculating the angle between it and the horizon with an instrument called a sextant, and then consulting constellation tables and making calculations, determine their boat's exact position.

Why would you need to bother, my daughter says, probably because I recently put a tracking app on her phone. One finger is all I need to locate her.

Because, I say, electronics can fail. The skills of the ancient navigators still come in handy, and only a fool would try to cross the ocean and refuse to learn them.

I explain how, on foggy days, their grandmother used a pair of calipers, a chart, and a parallel ruler to chart the course from whatever harbor we were in to the one we were trying to reach.

One summer, however, I say, we kept getting lost in the fog. But it wasn't her fault. The former owner, we finally figured out, had installed the compass too close to the engine, and it was scrambling the magnetism, and swinging the needle twenty degrees to the west. Pretty interesting, right?

No one finds this interesting, because they are asleep.

An hour later, the hotel looms high above the road on a treeless ridge. It's so sprawling, and has so many floors and staircases, and so defies logic, that the clerk provides, along with the room key, a floor plan.

My husband and daughter relax in the room while my son and I explore. He runs down a hallway, past a narrow staircase with an arrow and TOWER painted on the wall. He stops in front of the North Card Room, which indicates the likely existence of a South Card Room or an East or a West one, but according to the floor plan, there is only a North Card Room.

The door isn't locked. There's no fire in the fireplace, but the leather couches are warm, like giant, hibernating mammals, and the walls are lined with bookshelves.

The room feels hallowed and uncanny, as though a mysterious, celestial energy infuses it. I look at the floor plan. Viewed a certain way, every hallway emanates from this room.

This room is like the North Star of the hotel, I say. Do you know the other name for the North Star?

My son stalks the room, running his fingers over the thick, rounded book spines, their covers removed and the rough linen exposed. Scrape-silence, scrape-silence. His fingers fall quiet in the troughs.

It's Polaris, I say.

He finds a tiny leather briefcase on a bottom shelf.

Also, I say, the North Star isn't always the same star,

because the earth slowly bobbles on its axis. In fourteen
thousand years, Polaris will be replaced by the new
North Star, called Vega.

The briefcase's latch is stuck. Finally, he succeeds in
prying it open. Backgammon chips scatter everywhere.
Some land softly under the couch. Others click and
bounce on the stone hearth.

Points of orientation aren't constant, I say. They
change over time.

These sentences leave my mouth like a scold or a
warning or a lament. But he's too busy gathering the
far-flung discs, and stacking them back in the briefcase,
to register my sternness or sadness or both.

When I close the door to the North Card Room, the
lock trips, as if our entry was a time-space accident and
will never happen again.

My son runs down a minor flight of stairs, at the bottom of which is the Game Room. There's Ping-Pong and
pool and also arcade "games." One involves a metal claw
that hovers over a clear plastic box filled with plush animals that appear fluffily easy to nab. He begs for a dollar
to operate the claw. I refuse, but he cannot stop talking
about winning an animal. He wants one very, very badly.

After dinner, everyone goes to the Game Room. My
husband and I agree in advance: It's easier to give our
son five dollars, to spend however he likes, than to fend
off ceaseless requests to feed the claw. Before handing
him the money, my husband explains how the claw
works. It is not a game. It is a cash machine, but the

money goes in, not out. To engage with the cash machine is to consent to being manipulated. It is to believe, against all reason, that you can win when you can't. What he's paying for, thus, is false hope. He'd be better off spending his money on a game of pool or air hockey, where playing was the point, or as much the point, as winning or losing. Also, when his money is gone, he won't be getting any more.

My husband hands him the money. It's up to you, he says, how to best spend it.

Our son loses all five dollars to the claw within ninety seconds. He's crestfallen, yet still optimistic. He remains convinced of the inherent fairness of the claw. It *is* a game. You *can* win. My husband and I play air hockey, and try to lure him to watch, but no matter where anyone stands in the Game Room, the claw box with its candy-colored animals glows in the periphery, lit up like a diner and making me hungry even though we just ate. I refuse to find metaphoric the way the claw is shiny, and possibly greased. It's probably no coincidence that just beyond the claw is the Sweets Shop, which has rock walls like a cave and is warmly lit, as though by the very fire that allowed our ancestors to survive. Although initially the hotel felt poorly imagined—large hallways ending at tiny staircases that lead nowhere—I now see that it's brilliantly imagined, each seemingly stumbled-upon nook cueing a different anxiety or desire that must, with money, be quelled. And yet I also know that's not exactly the case. The hotel is a "gump job," as my boatbuilder neighbor might say. The original hotel plan—a copy of the 1923 architectural drawings hangs in the lobby—did not age well. Future needs emerged that the building contorted itself to meet, and so the basement became a Game Room and the root cellar became a Sweets Shop and the library became a Martini Bar and the attic became a Pedicure Spa and the South, West, and East Card Rooms became Business Centers. The hotel, like the trees outside our apartment, the ones in the median pummeled by the relentless wind of speeding trucks, has been buffeted by human desire— and has buffeted it—and so feels intentionally shaped and yet not, because no one person is to be "blamed" or credited for the fact that there's a claw in the basement of a nineteenth-century hotel, nor that my son is now seething to possess a purple polyester animal that isn't even cute. I've carefully shaped and curated this weekend, I've exposed my children to oldness and strangeness and the Gothic promise of danger at the turn of every hallway, but instead, here we are, staring at unwinnable animals in a scratched Plexiglas box, quickly doomed, if sprung, for a landfill.

On the way to the Sweets Shop, our son begs for one last chance at the claw. My husband relents and gives him a dollar. Maybe this time he'll finally *finally* learn that he'll never win at this game, and apparently he has learned something, because he hands his last chance to his sister.

She beats the game and the predictions, and pro-
cures, for her brother, a purple dog.

There's barely any internet in the room. The TV gets
only a handful of channels. One exclusively runs shows
about Americans, usually white and straight and more
often than not Southern but sometimes Midwestern or
from Vegas, buying and renovating houses.

The show that's on tonight, episode following episode
following episode, is about American couples moving
temporarily to Europe. The four of us crowd onto the
bed to watch a husband and wife from Ohio choose
among three apartments in Brussels. The husband
wants a home that resembles an extended-stay motel
suite. The wife wants a home with "character" close to
town so she can people-watch in cafés. They haggle over
cost, meaning the wife wants to spend more than the
husband does, and he keeps reminding her of their budget, even though the apartment he wants is also over
budget.

The husband gets his way.

The next episode is about an American couple in
Paris. The wife wants a garret apartment with a hot
plate kitchen and a view of the Eiffel Tower; the husband wants a building with underground parking in a
charmless neighborhood near the airport. The husband
gets his way. In the next episode, the American couple is
in Amsterdam. She wants the seventeenth-century
apartment on the canal. He wants the contemporary

house forty-five minutes from the city. The husband gets his way.

Following the third episode, my husband summarizes the fake conflict that drives the show prior to the inevitable moment when the husband gets his way, and the wife pretends she also chose the apartment that represents everything she dislikes.

He wants clean lines. She wants cozy.

Everybody laughs, including me. In our apartment I can't stop putting pillows on all the furniture, and my husband can't stop hiding them behind the couch when I go out of town.

In Rome, a wife finally gets her way. The husband agrees to live in a thickly curtained apartment near the Trevi Fountain. Suddenly, I see the rhythm, the strategy. This show is the claw. Every once in a rare while, it defies expectations and undermines its critics with a strategically placed anomaly.

Everyone gets ready for bed. My son and daughter share the pull-out couch. I stay awake and read my phone in the dark, but then I hear rustling. My son can't sleep. Outside, an animal is making noises that sound like it's dying.

I walk him to the window. If we can see where the sound is coming from, he might be less scared. But there's no precise source. Instead, the entire horizon is a violin string activated by an invisible bow.

The stars are very bright.

That's Vega, I say.

He seems to never have heard of Vega.

Remember? I say. Eventually, it will be the new North Star.

This seems like an uplifting note on which to end the day.

That's sad, he says.

Why sad? I ask.

It seems he's referring to whatever animal is mating, or grieving, in the dark. Maybe if I draw the heavy drapes, the room will become like the Roman apartment, the outside world muffled. The anomaly is cozy. She wants anomalies.

Because, he says. Then no one will care about the old one.

The storm is due in a few hours. My husband lifts pans and hats on the kitchen counter, searching for the car keys. He's headed to the store, at my request, to get emergency supplies. Inspired panic is not his go-to response, but it's also possible, as can happen when time is tight and labor divided, that I'd already claimed the role of giddy cataclysmist. In the interests of eliminating redundancies, he'd found a different area in which to excel.

He asks if there's anything else "we" need. He wants me to know: I'm not alone while preparing for the future, planning for its storms and guests.

I fill the bathtub in case the electricity fails, because

it's too much of a pain to haul the concrete top off the well and throw a bucket down the hole.

My son, meanwhile, waits outside. He's dragged an old mooring ball out of the bamboo. The ball is made of hard plastic and trails a dirty piece of rope. He yells to hurry up, but I can't hurry the water out of the ground and through the pipes. Besides, the house is making a strange noise. The house is constantly making noises— the well pump, the furnace, the sump pump. Normally, clicking is followed by a deeper silence that immediately proceeds the groan of old machines heaving into action.

But today the clicks sound too faint, and the groan is too high-pitched.

The basement is through a hole in a closet floor. The dirt down here smells clean, of minerals. No sunlight has struck it for two centuries. Multiple old furnaces and oil tanks lurk in one corner. How they got down here is a mystery, because they're too large to be removed.

Once at the bottom of the stairs I can tell from the location of the noise: There's a problem with the well pump again. This is both good news and bad. There's no fixing this pump, or rather, the fix is a trick. The pump must be tricked into forgetting it's broken.

All that's required is a quick flip of the breaker. Off, on.

By the time the tub is filled, my son is jumping with the mooring ball on the trampoline. This seems like a terrible idea until we devise a game, with rules and scoring. He's winning by five points when the mooring ball takes a wrong bounce and nearly knocks out his front tooth.

Back inside, he lies on a couch and holds an ice cube to his lip. He's suspiciously sheepish for the victim of an accident. Then his face contorts. He's clearly trying to hide an object in his mouth. How long has that object been in there? I don't need to ask because the answer is a long time, many hours, probably since he woke up. He's nearly seven years old yet still behaves like a toddler, sucking on pennies, screws, the tiny plastic detritus he finds on the sidewalk or on the kitchen floor, such as those rings that prove the milk hasn't been opened by a stranger, and which somehow never make it into the trash.

He surrenders a paper clip on his tongue. But confessing to guilt isn't enough. He must endure an interrogation where the only way to evade punishment is to answer none of the following questions: Why was he jumping on the trampoline while chewing on a paper clip? Why, after his death has been graphically described to him, as though he's a jury convened to self-convict, does he continue to put small objects in his mouth? Why doesn't he just chew his shirt or suck his thumb or adopt any number of habits that won't lead to his extinction?

He plays with my phone and I take it away. He plays with my hair clip and I take it away. He pokes through the ziplock bag of blank Annunciation painting postcards I bought at the barn sale almost a year ago, and which I'd forgotten about until they recently appeared between two coffee-table books. Why the original owner collected them is far less mysterious than why I bought them.

He studies a postcard where a woman is hiding behind a table because a little boy wearing a dress broke into her house.

What's happening here? he asks.

Though a person with two literature degrees, I've never read the Bible. I have tried. The same year I received the Greek myths book, I'd also received a book of Bible stories for children that had all of the relationship drama of a math worksheet and so could not compare. As an adult, I've tried to read Genesis multiple times, but God too much resembles the childless Hungarian heiress who runs an artists' retreat out of her ancestral castle, and who, I've heard, since I've never been invited, pits friends against one another until they become rivals, and spreads false rumors and sows discord, all for her own entertainment. I once took my son to one of the parties the heiress sometimes throws in her stateside pied-à-terre, because he was six days old and asleep most hours of the day in what was basically a soft, over-the-shoulder purse, but was warned, by a friend, not to do this, because the heiress "would never take me seriously," and never invite me to her castle, if she knew I had a baby. At her house, I saw faded photos of her when young, holding a small, white-haired child.

I've never received God's call, or hers.

The Annunciation, however, is a Bible story I know.

First, I tell my son what a virgin is.

That's an important part to the story, I say. It's one of the reasons she's so famous.

I summarize the plot. The Virgin Mary had a husband named Joseph. The two of them wanted children but for some reason they couldn't. God decided to help by giving them a baby, but rather than just delivering it to them, and sparing the Virgin Mary the pain and risk of childbirth, which would have seemed completely within his power to do, instead, and without her permission, he magically impregnated her, and then sent a young angel named Gabriel to tell her what he'd done.

My son flips to a different postcard, where Mary is bent at the waist, her hands crossed over her abdomen as though she's got a cramp.

She doesn't look very happy, he says.

She does not. Also, this Bible story I thought I knew suddenly makes no sense.

If Mary was Joseph's wife, I say, thinking aloud, and they wanted a baby, how was it possible that Mary was still a virgin?

I'm irritated in a circular, inescapable way, as I get when I can't locate my phone, a thing that's used to locate.

Maybe Mary wasn't a virgin, my son says. Maybe that was just her name.

The word *virgin* sounds so adorable coming out of

[handwritten margin note: X — not an infertility narrative — Mary was a teen + they were engaged but not yet married]

his mouth; it's no more freighted with adult meaning than the words *parrot* or *popsicle*. But the word also makes my lower back tingle, because I can too easily imagine a time in the future when I'll feel differently. This word coming out of his mouth will be more like an object that should not be there, a safety pin or penny. I can easily imagine this future because it happened the other day when he returned from his friend's house with the word *sluts* in his mouth. He was so excited to share with me what had happened. His friend's older brother was making fun of a boy in his grade who loved musicals and was only friends with girls. The brother said of this boy, according to my son, *He hangs out with sluts!*

My son laughed as the brother had laughed, and as he clearly expected me to laugh, too.

After dinner that night, I'd consulted with my husband. Clearly, I said, if the two of us don't pay close attention, our small boy might call girls sluts so his friends would like him better, and then, over time, he might come to think that girls *were* sluts, maybe especially the ones who refused to have sex with him.

My husband, as always, remained circumspect. He trusted that, through example and education—and by staying vigilant—the two of us could limit certain negative outcomes and help him sort through the many competing messages the world can send a small boy on his way to adulthood.

His measured strategy seemed the more useful, less reactionary one. And yet it didn't make me feel any more confident that we knew what we were doing, or that we would or should succeed.

The next day, I'd asked my son to sit next to me on the couch. About yesterday, I said. I want to talk about the story you told me about the brother.

I asked him if he knew what the word *sluts* meant. He either didn't know, or figured it was better to pretend that he didn't.

Let's look it up, I said.

According to my phone, I said, a slut is "a woman who has many casual sex partners."

So, I said. This definition implies a lot that isn't stated. Conventionally, when a female is called a slut, it's an insult meant to suggest that, based on antique notions of female sexuality, she has "low morals" and is "easy," thus cheapening her value in the marriage economy and exposing her to other dangers, such as being blamed for crimes when she is, in fact, their victim. Males, when they are called sluts, are more conventionally being congratulated, because their ability to have sex with many people is seen as proof of their irresistibility, vigor, and skill. To be fair, a male slut might also limit his options in the relationship economy. His potential mates might be wisely warned away. But he can always change, and his past will not follow him into the future, and whoever presides over his change will be seen as powerful. The reformed male slut, in other words, confers value on the reformer, as well as on himself, and poses no ongoing reputational risk to any person who bravely dares to love him.

Are you following me so far? I asked.

He nodded.

However, I said, the situation with your friend's brother seems even a bit more complicated. That the boy was only friends with girls, and not boys, and was obsessed by musicals, meant that he wasn't, perhaps, conforming to the brother's idea of how a male his age should behave and what should matter to him. For whatever reason, the boy's difference was something the brother needed to belittle him for, and given he clearly understood that "sluts" was an insult, he thus assumed that to accuse a person of hanging out with them was also an insult, even if it was highly unlikely for these nine-year-old girls to be sluts, if a slut was defined as "a woman who has many casual sex partners."

Regardless, I said, what concerns me is how, without really knowing how to use the word *sluts* correctly, by which I mean in the "conventionally offensive" manner, the brother was communicating what he believed, or what he believed he should believe, about males who weren't acting in a way he understood as acceptable, and thus the boy needed to be teased, or corrected, and this was best accomplished by also demeaning females, whose taint, in his understanding, was contagious.

Does that make sense to you? I said.

But even as I asked this question, I wasn't sure that I

made sense to myself, or that I had any idea what I was talking about, or that I hadn't just made things worse.

My son seemed smaller than when we began this conversation. He'd started to sink into the space between the couch cushions that hides crumbs and money.

Am I in trouble? he asked.

The storm is getting closer. The wind sounds like a large creature hurling itself against the house, trying to get in. The elm makes ticktock noises as its giant branches swing.

On the wall opposite the couch hangs a shadow box my mother found while deaccessioning during their recent move. The plaque reads, FOREIGN BODIES REMOVED FROM THE FOOD AND AIR PASSAGES BY WILSON JAMES TROUP MD OF THE GREEN BAY CLINIC, GREEN BAY, WISCONSIN.

Wilson J. Troup was my grandfather. Tacked inside is a piece of paper with a typewritten caption: *The youngest patient was a girl five months of age, who swallowed the small open safety pin. The oldest was a woman seventy-six years of age, who swallowed the flat chicken bone.*

The bones have turned rusty. They shed beige grit. The coins are black and the button tarnished. I often call my son's attention to the shadow box whenever a foreign body is discovered in his mouth, though the message he receives from the shadow box is apparently the opposite of what I intend. The message he receives is that he can put all the foreign bodies in his mouth that he wants, and he will always be saved.

The wind smacks the house again. The elm branches count the seconds up, or down.

I pull the shadow box off the wall and lay it across our laps. I point to a button, a tiny silver dog charm, a skate key.

This shadow box, I say, is like the trash heap in the backyard. When it rains hard, or the wind really blows, the heap disgorges a new trove of curiosities, bottle caps and bean cans and broken forks, and all of these objects suggest who used to live in this house and what they did in these rooms. Likewise, I say, if a person looked closely at the items in this shadow box, they could learn a lot about the people of Green Bay, Wisconsin, circa 1955, and what they put in their mouths and why.

The windows rattle in their casings. My son flinches. The vibrations of the approaching storm enter the house and the bodies of the people in the house.

Here is how, I say, pulling him close, the people of Green Bay nearly came to ruin. The people of Green Bay loved to tell jokes over a meal and throw their heads back and laugh with their maws full of bony food. The people of Green Bay, whose eyesight was failing, could recall the shape of the charms on their favorite bracelet only if they put them under their tongues and fell asleep remembering. Spare change needed to be hidden from the burglars, who liked to surprise the people of Green Bay by peeking in the windows and loudly blowing a kazoo. The children of Green Bay who broke toys knew to hide the evidence of their crimes in their mouths, and tried, unsuccessfully, to reach adulthood undiscovered. Older boys told younger boys to store their skate keys in their cheeks while they raced downhill. Older boys told younger boys to slip safety pins into the sandwiches of their adversaries. Older boys told younger boys that whenever they saw lightning and had a silver button in their mouths, the smart thing to do was swallow.

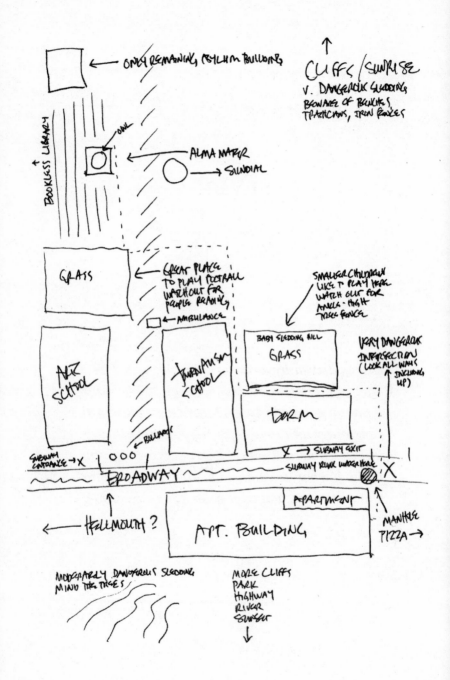

SEVEN

Unless driven by stress of weather, avoid this harbor. It is large, commercial, dirty, and without good landing places. Its waters are constantly agitated by ferries, fishermen, and large steamers. Tankers go right through the main harbor to the oil wharves. If you do choose to visit, however, lie on the eastern side.

After town, and just past the muddy inlet where people set up easels to paint the sunset, a road cuts sharply uphill to the left. Most people park near the barn that almost burned down last year when two nine-year-old boys, on a rainy day, sat in the empty hayloft, and rather than tossing a ball to each other, threw lit matches instead.

Everyone is on the screened porch because it rained an hour ago and the mosquitoes are fierce. A friend urges me to introduce myself to the famous writer who recently won an important prize and is currently braving the bugs while straddling a stone wall, the other side of which drops steeply toward the woods. From a distance, he appears to be yelling at a young couple, but

that doesn't mean he's angry. He's known for his ambi-
ent as well as his actual rage; sometimes he seems like
he's playing a role he created when he was younger, and
now he's stuck with this character until he dies.

The grass is still wet. Rain sticks to my ankles and
makes them itch. In theory, I don't need to introduce
myself to the famous writer, because we've met before,
but each time we reencounter each other, he needs to
be reminded who I am. Much like a certain friend of
mine who demands I do chores for her, because this is
how intimacy on her terms is achieved, perhaps the famous writer believes that the best way for him to get to
know someone is to perpetually greet them as a stranger.

As I approach, I hear him announcing to the couple
that writers should never have children because each
child represents a book the writer will not write.

Though the writer is doing nothing more harmful
than perpetuating his brand, it's hard, once I arrive at
the wall, not to want to litigate his claims. The famous
writer flicks his eyes over me—he clearly recognizes
me—but instead of acknowledging that we've met or
pretending that we haven't, continues to offer wisdom
that isn't wisdom so much as his life repackaged as a
universal truth.

The woman and the man politely nod, maybe in gen-
uine agreement, maybe to keep the famous writer from
directing his intensity at them, as he warns of the dangers they *must*, if they wish to pursue a life of the mind,
avoid.

By his own logic, however, the famous writer—who has no children and has written ten books—would have had ten children if he'd written no books. I consider asking him if conservative politicians should campaign against people writing books in the same way that they campaign against people getting abortions, because each book represents a life that could have happened but didn't.

But sometimes it's more valuable to let a person uninterruptedly talk, because despite what my great-uncle said about me, I really do listen. If you listen, you can hear warnings. Whenever we got lost in the fog on *Second Chance,* my mother carefully monitored the depth sounder, because land could sneak up from below. Soundings approximated a map of the ocean floor, although the map wasn't the important thing, the distance *from* the map was the important thing. Fifty feet. Twenty. Ten. When the map got too close, an alarm went off. The soundings made a sound.

I've learned, from listening, as though I'm a human depth sounder using sonar to see if there's enough water to pass, when it isn't worth running aground with certain people, and when I shouldn't waste my breath.

While I don't deny that children require an immeasurable and sometimes debilitating amount of time and effort and money and emotional labor, so do a lot of things. This is not to say that everyone—or even anyone—should have children, but more to wonder why children are so often cited as the predominant menace to artistic self-fulfillment. Meaning, even while I would never recommend or even suggest that people have children, I can still be suspicious of what the equation (one book = one child) covertly implies. I'm especially suspicious where the famous writer is concerned. He reminds me of a composer friend who said of his children, now adults, *they were my wife's idea.* His wife and her ideas were the opponents of his art. After he lost the war against them, he was too weakened by defeat, apparently, to do much childcare. Still, he suffered. I have little doubt that the famous writer would have spent comparatively little time raising the children he never had. What he's communicating when he says one child equals one book is his need to be the only dependent in his household, and the only person for whom his partner exclusively cares, otherwise he, and by extension his art, will suffer.

The bugs swarm more thickly—the half hour between sundown and total darkness is when their armies fully mobilize—and the famous writer becomes enraged trying to fend them off. He's basically punching himself in the face. Eventually, he stalks off, affronted, as if he's been singled out by nature and unfairly attacked. The couple follows him through the door with the screen that someone's baby broke, because every baby costs one screen door. Inside, the dinner is arranged in a circle on the table, meat, beans, bread, potatoes, salad, dessert. The food sketches out a compass rose, the chocolate cake marking magnetic north. The needles of the children are drawn toward it. My mother, one summer, taught me how to plot a course and calculate the difference between true and magnetic north. True north is the north pole. Magnetic north is the point where the lines of the earth's magnetic field, which flow south-north and north-south, converge. The charts my mother used noted the degree of magnetic declination for our area. These degrees needed to be added or subtracted before settling on a heading. Since magnetic north was discovered in 1831, its location has traveled 1,400 miles. North is not a place, it's a runaway. Charts need to be updated every seven years to keep pace with it. The phone I use to find my daughter has a compass. It corrects for magnetic declination, but similar to a boat engine, a phone's magnetic field can warp a reading. So can a city. A phone cannot be used to navigate precisely. A phone can be used to approximately locate a daughter. *Your friend is somewhere in the circle.*

Back outside on the patio is a chair missing an arm, because due to babies, neglect, weather, many of the chairs are busted and listing. The famous writer stands under the bug zapper, buttonholing a young woman about children and books. He seems to have picked up where he left off, unaware that his audience has changed. Why, I wonder, as I sit on the flagstones, which are densely cold, as though presaturated with the dropping nighttime temperatures, is the famous writer so committed to this cause? Why do children, and by his implication women, pose the greatest threat to his creative output? Why doesn't the famous writer think of eating in terms of books he'll never write, or bathing or sleeping or getting dressed?

If I were his life accountant, I'd invite him to my office, look at his daily existence returns, and say to him, *Let's run the numbers.*

Having a child, I would tell him, will require roughly seven years of his life. As I could personally attest, by the age of seven a child can become no more emotionally demanding than laundry. This presumes, of course, that the famous writer has an equal domestic partner, which he does, and can afford a lot of childcare, which he can, and lets the child watch a lot of TV, which I would recommend.

Whereas, I'd say, if he were to reduce his sleep by four hours per night, he could gain two months per year, and if he stops cooking food to eat on plates that he will then have to wash, he could, if the market were strong, gain an additional two months per year. However, if he persists in sleeping and eating as he's been doing, then over the course of nine years, he will spend the same amount of time sleeping and eating as I've spent coraising a child to the laundry phase of existence, meaning that he will have cost himself one book in addition to roughly $250,000 in childcare expenses. If his career lasts fifty years, then due to sleeping and eating, he will fail to write 5.6 books. I have two children (-2), but because of them I don't sleep or have any time to cook or eat (+5.6). So, I will have cost myself, in addition to a quarter of a million dollars, only 3.6 books.

Children, according to the spreadsheet, which, true, puts me massively in the red, actually helped me write *more* books than the famous writer, because I was forced to live without his seemingly necessary, but actually, according to the numbers, totally luxurious approach to sleeping and eating.

Then I would lean back in my office chair and speak so softly that the famous writer had to lean close to hear me.

I just want you to be aware of the choices you've made, I'd say, based on beliefs you might not even know you have. You should ask yourself why you wouldn't choose differently about eating and sleeping if the costs are so dear.

The famous writer suddenly looks in my direction. His eyes are ice-blue and his reptilian intelligence cuts across the patio. He keeps staring, as though trying to remember where he's seen me before—he's already forgotten the encounter at the stone wall—and suddenly I feel outed, my hypocrisy exposed. Because I've also fallen prey to these beliefs or fears, if collaterally. My body, to others, I'd believed, was the enemy of my mind; I'd sacrificed all my ideas because I had this one idea. For this reason, I kept my first pregnancy a secret. I'm ashamed, now, that I did this, even while I had what seemed like valid reasons at the time. My best friend, an academic, became pregnant just before I did, and she didn't have tenure yet, and she'd told me how a childless superior in her department said to her, *I guess you're not serious about your career.* I didn't want anyone to think I wasn't serious about my career. I'd laughed at myself afterward and made myself into a running joke. I believed I could prevent people from ever knowing I had a baby! I'd hide it for eighteen years, after which it would be out of the house! If I were to visit a life accountant, my spreadsheet might reveal the following. While I've never, to my knowledge, experienced the professional cost of having a child—because I can afford to hire other people to mind them, and because my husband, in addition to doing half the childcare, doesn't act like a neglected child when I pay attention to our actual children—I have experienced the unceasing pressure of proving that, by having a child, I've cost myself nothing, and this has cost me.

Dessert is being served in the dining room. The patio empties out. Suddenly, the boys who nearly set the barn on fire scurry past in a military hunch, trying to evade detection by fake combatants, unless I'm the combatant, in which case their mission has already failed. The two of them stand on top of the stone wall and take turns pushing each other off. The drop on the other side is at least four feet. Their bodies are silent when they hit the ground. Then they climb the wall and push each other off again.

Soon, my son appears.

One boy says to the other, Who is she?

They let him join them on the wall, but a slight suspicion remains.

This is one of those moments when I should maybe intervene. The impact of the fall might be too much for his smaller body to absorb. But I decide to give it a few minutes, to run a risk assessment before ruining his fun. The three of them, meanwhile, become more and more excited by the falling variations they create and the different ways of fake-killing one another. Stabbing. Strangulation. The older boys are full of ideas that my son is thrilled to adopt. Not all of these ideas are good ones. The same is true of my ideas. If, as a thought experiment, I were to accept the famous writer's claim that one child equals one book, the math becomes confused when a person writes a book about a child. How to calculate that cost? Are the gains or losses exponential?

The older boys, meanwhile, have made their hands into guns, and moved north along the wall, where the drop is more extreme. My son watches, fascinated, as one boy shoots himself in the face and vanishes over the edge. The boy yells as his body strikes an object that, from my chair, I can't see. Before I can stop him, my son takes his place on the wall, and points his finger at his head, and shoots.

This bar, so close to the banks, is usually full of suited men whose soft bodies expand and contract when they laugh, the scene, at a squint, resembling an underwater reef covered by pulsing, dark anemones.

But not tonight. Tonight, the bar is empty. My friend and I order drinks and snacks and fill in each other's life blanks, since we haven't seen each other in a few years. She's a professional mediator specializing in workplace discrimination. Her job can be emotionally draining, but she's always, until recently, managed to compartmentalize.

Six months ago, however, she says, I was hired to mediate a situation where the female employees felt discriminated against by their boss. A week after accepting the job, I learned that this boss was the son of a long-ago friend.

The bartender sets two places and puts a tea light between the napkins. He's slow about it, and clearly eavesdropping, in search of an opening so he can join our conversation and become our temporary ally. Establishing transient intimacy is part of his job. He's also made it clear: He pled our case to the kitchen, which had just closed when we arrived. They stayed open for us because of his advocacy.

We are starving and genuinely grateful.

When this friend learned that I was the mediator in her son's case, she says, she left me messages at work. When I graciously refused, through my assistant, to speak with her, she sent a long email about how nice, decent, and fair her son was, and how she hoped that I might remember the time we'd all gone to the beach, when her son was nine, and he'd saved a wounded seagull from being killed by a dog.

I consider, for half a second, asking my friend if I can see this email. Bars used to be where I flirted and seduced; now they're the sites of illicit document exchange. A different friend had recently shared, in the unlit, sticky corner of a bar, the legal complaint submitted by her soon-to-be-ex-husband's lawyer, which read like a novel narrated by a paranoid protagonist. In this protagonist's version, she'd lived off his money and stolen his ideas. The clothes on her back and the thoughts in her head. All belonged to him.

I recused myself from the job, she says, which I should have done immediately. I thought I could be impartial, but after she sent me that email, I definitely knew I couldn't be.

Because the case she made for her son was so convincing? I ask.

It was actually pretty generic, she said. Expressions of love for one's children tend to all sound the same.

She smiles as though she knows that I agree with her, and I guess I probably do.

But the effect her email had on me was definitely not generic, she says. It made me angry. I felt compelled by it to do unethical things, like break confidentiality. I desperately wanted to write back and tell this friend what I knew about her son. I'd seen the evidence and conducted the preliminary interviews. He was far from fair or decent. I experienced a nearly deranging urge to enlighten her or scold her. I was so furious at her for her naïveté. How could she not see who her son really was? Surely there'd been signs.

Maybe he became this person as an adult, I say. Maybe he was changed by whatever happened to him after he left home.

Maybe, she says. But then my reaction became a mirror in which I saw an unflattering version of myself. Her son also has a father. Why wasn't I mad at him?

My friend doesn't look down, or away, as if I'm also a mirror she's peering into.

Do you know the father? I ask.

Not really, she says. But that's not the point, is it? Afterward, I talked with my therapist about how I'd reacted. Instinctually, where I'd placed the blame. Eventually she asked me, "Do you take credit for your son?"

How did you answer? I say.

I don't think she meant it as a question, she says. I was just supposed to think about it. If I took the credit, then would I implicitly have to take the blame?

She finally breaks eye contact, and takes a long, slow sip of her drink, as if thinking about it still.

If your son were accused by a co-worker of discrimination or harassment, I say, how would you respond?

The bartender sets at a diagonal, above our plates, a skinny wooden board full of meat and shiny nuts. He's given up trying to befriend us through talking. Instead, he establishes intimacy through gestures. He holds up a wine bottle and raises his eyebrows. I nod and he refills.

Probably the best way for me to answer that question, she says, is by describing two situations, neither of which has to do with the workplace, but both of which have to do with the challenge of whom to believe.

When I was in college, she says, I had a roommate who went to a party with the goal of seducing a particular man. She'd even made a bet with another of our friends. If she succeeded, this friend would owe her twenty dollars. That night, at the party, she flirted and danced with the man and eventually he invited her back to his room. They started to kiss on his bed, and then he flipped her over, and tore her dress, and fucked her roughly from behind.

The next morning, she says, when my roommate told me what happened, I urged her to file a report with our college. But my roommate insisted that the man was responding to what he understood as her desires and how to satisfy them, and so even if he'd taken some liberties she'd rather he hadn't, she didn't feel he was criminally at fault.

For the rest of the semester, she says, I kept encouraging my roommate to report the man to the school, or at least to see a counselor. Our friendship became more and more strained. Just before we graduated, she and I had an ugly fight. She accused me of disrespecting and even negating her, by not believing her account. I told her that I'd only wanted to support her, but truthfully I *was* frustrated with her. Why wouldn't she confront what had happened to her and at least get help?

She pauses to fill her plate.

It seems this is a trend with me, she says.

What? I say.

Getting angry at women for the behavior of men, she says.

The bartender returns. He tops off our wine this time without even asking, and then gives me a look to make his message clear: *This is on the house.* I remember this trick from my decade of waiting tables. We'd give the customers free or extra food and drinks, we'd imply that we especially liked them and favored them over all of our other customers, and they would give us bigger tips. It was stealing in the guise of hospitality, which also didn't feel like stealing, since the owners paid us far below minimum wage. The owners knew but pretended not to know we did this. They'd factored both their ethical lapses and ours into their business plan.

Isn't it a bit more complicated than that? I say.

Is it? she says.

Your roommate was protecting a man to protect herself, I say.

Right, she says. In order to save herself she had to harbor a criminal. Not that I'm blaming her. I'm just stating a fact.

She drains a third of her wine.

So that's the first situation, she says. Here is the second.

About a month ago, she says, I was contacted by a twenty-three-year-old man. To the degree that anyone so much younger than myself could be a friend, I count him as one, though I'm really more like a proxy parent, since his are dead, and the grandmother who raised him lives thousands of miles away. He's exceptionally smart and ambitious and charming and funny. He's also rich. He invented a few apps before graduating from college and founded a startup. While clearly a prodigy in some areas, on the relationship front he was totally inexperienced. But then he met a woman at an office party. They talked for hours on a couch. He liked her so much, and their connection was so easy and felt so familiar, that he imagined, before he'd even kissed her, they might become a couple. At 2 AM, they went back to his apartment and had sex. The next morning, she left in a hurry. She refused, for a week, to return his texts. He was in a panic. Was his inexperience a turnoff? Her silence made him deeply insecure, and so he stopped contacting her. A month or so later, the woman told a mutual friend that he'd taken advantage of her drunkenness and forced her to have sex with him. She wrote about him on social media. He was now being pressured by his investors to resign.

The bartender floats past with his bottle. He raises his eyebrows. When I don't respond, he nods once and moves on.

At first, my friend says, when the young man called me in a scared, confused panic, I, too, was scared and panicky. Even though I've never met or spoken with the woman, her behavior suggested that whatever happened at his apartment had deeply and immediately devastated her. At the same time, I couldn't imagine the young man *I* knew taking advantage of a person against their will. I spent days arguing both sides with myself. Whom to believe, the man or the woman? It wore me down; I wanted to *decide* and be done thinking about it. The easiest solution was to conclude that I'd been wrong about the young man. He was capable of selfish, violent, criminal acts, and I was just a terrible judge of character. But to decide that he was a deceitful person who'd duped me was actually a way of letting myself off the hook, by turning myself into another of his victims. I owed it to both the woman, and the man, to exist a bit longer in this uncomfortable space. Finally, I came up with a way to explain how the young man—the one I knew—could have done what the woman alleged.

Her voice is so loud, suddenly. I wonder if she's had too much to drink. Then I notice. The bartender has turned the music off.

Given his guilelessness and his excitability, she says, I could imagine a situation where he didn't perceive a boundary. Personality traits such as enthusiasm, tenacity, persuasiveness, an ability to "make things happen," and "never take no for an answer," were lauded by universities and the business world, both places to which he'd fought to gain access, because as a child, raised in a rural town of four hundred by his grandmother, without any connections or means, he'd had none. He'd mastered that value system and wildly succeeded, yet by applying the same strategies to the bedroom, he'd failed to hear what the woman was telling him.

The bartender places a vinyl billfold between our half-full glasses. I slip my card inside and hand it back. He returns with the billfold and a pen, which he places at an angle, so that it will be easy for me to pick it up. The more interactions we have without speaking, the more intimate our faux relationship becomes. I remember this, too, from waiting tables. To connect wordlessly with a total stranger made me feel flirty, savvy, and primal. I was practicing the art of prelingual communication while running a scam.

Also, to clarify, she says, I'm not excusing or exonerating his behavior. I just wanted to understand how two totally different versions of this young man can exist.

The bartender raises the lights to signal us to leave. I sign and add the requisite extra money to his tip. I hope that number says to him: In the absence of a more transparent and worker-friendly economy, I support your act of theft. More likely he'll think that he fooled us, that we have no idea what happens in bars, when the lights are on or when they're off.

But perhaps that's the flaw in my thinking, my friend says, as she puts on her coat. To persist in seeing him as two people, rather than one.

On the corner of 101st Street is the playground with a hollow pyramid covered with slick, orange tiles. Here, a child can still chip a tooth or fall through the small hole in the top of the pyramid and drop fifteen feet to the ground. A child can still slip on the metal ladder that seams the narrow shaft.

My daughter sits on a swing with her phone while I hang from the monkey bars to stretch my back. My son, on top of the pyramid, climbs into the hole. Hardly anyone is in the park besides us. Rain is predicted in an hour.

A nearby street lamp flickers on and off. The wind, as the storm front approaches, starts to gust, as though the atmosphere is trying to catch its breath. These gusts are colder than the air around them, because the weather is pressing down from the north, from Canada, maybe even the Arctic. The cold is an advance warning of what's to come. Fog, I remember, sent similar warnings. Up to an hour before it arrived, I could sense the faint electric prickles on my cheek, the summer air suddenly smelling like snow.

This wind, however, is more like a chilly slap, and the smell is dry, with the sweetness of garbage. Still, when I shut my eyes, I can imagine I'm with my brother on the foredeck of *Second Chance* searching for the geometric specters of red nuns and green cans. The colors and shapes (nuns are pointed; cans have a flat top) marked the ledges we didn't want to hit. They outlined the safe passage. *Red right return* is the nautical shorthand; keep the red nun to starboard as you're coming back into the harbor, and the green cans to port. But *red right return* presumes you know in which direction home lies. In the Reach, a stretch of water with two open ends, return is hard to distinguish from departure.

But my brother and I, when we were on the foredeck, used all of our senses. We listened for seals or birds, and also for bells, because certain aids use sound to help people find them. The bells hung inside cylindrical cages that rolled on top of the waves. The motion caused a hectic clanging that, in high seas, made the bell seem as if it belonged to a clock tower struggling to count each sped-up hour as the world careered toward the end.

Unfortunately, when the sea was flat, which it often

was in the fog, the bells made scarcely any noise at all. And so, my brother and I had to carefully listen for the hesitant and erratic *tings,* nearly indistinguishable from the drops of condensation collecting on the stays and the mast spreaders that, at irregular intervals, shook free and landed on our heads.

The sky starts to heavily mist. We need to cross the park before we get drenched. On the other side is a museum exhibit that nobody except me wants to see. But I've told my son and daughter about the museum's gift shop, which sells toys with no apparent connection to the art on the walls save a pragmatic one: The toys are a bribe that enables those who want to see the art to see it.

My son runs ahead. He's our advance team. My daughter and I follow at a more relaxed pace. The park was designed to force people to meander. Unlike the city grid that surrounds it, the paths here loop south and north as they slowly head east between the granite outcroppings that appear, through the drizzle, like tiny, haunted mountains.

Ahead, I notice a man. He's standing and watching my son battle an invisible opponent, punching and kicking at nothing.

He poses no immediate danger to my son—he's stooped and probably in his seventies, I think my daughter and I could take him—but for some reason I hear ringing in my head a caution issued by my friend's uncle. This uncle is about the same age as this stranger. One night, I was with the uncle on an island. A few families had rowed out to watch the twilight. My son was more interested in disturbing the pink, reflective water by bombing it with rocks. *You need to watch out for him,* the uncle said, with ominous certainty. If my son were older, the uncle might have been warning me that my son, rocks in hand, posed a danger to others. But since he was only seven, the caution more likely implied that he was the one in danger. I understood what he meant without him needing to say it. But what led the uncle to this conclusion? Was it because my son was a long-haired boy, or because he's mistaken for a girl? Furthermore, where did the uncle's authority come from? Had he been a victim once himself? Or did he find himself tempted to create them?

Regardless, his somber tone suggested: He knew, firsthand, the hazards posed by certain men.

Maybe this man, currently observing my son throw punches in the park, is one of the men the uncle was warning me about.

The man hears our footsteps and stiffens when he sees us. Then he walks toward us, chest newly inflated with authority, as though he's a park ranger about to write us a ticket.

She sure has a lot of energy, he says, sounding a lot like my other grandfather, the one who worked as a foreman in a typewriter factory. Everything this grandfather said, even when complimentary, hid a critique. He developed Alzheimer's in his seventies. In his final decade, whenever my grandmother and I sat around re-membering the fun times I'd spent at their house before he got sick, he'd listen with a skeptical look on his face, and then, after the story was over, say, *I'm glad I wasn't there.*

Actually, my daughter says to the man, he's a boy.

The man scrutinizes my son in the distance. Then he looks at my daughter, and at me.

No, he says, she's not.

We watch him hurry away, forgoing the looping path and cutting a straight line toward the apartment build-ings that mark the park's western border like geometric cliffs. I could use this as a teaching moment, the lesson reducible to a single sentence. *What an asshole that guy is.*

Instead, my daughter sees an opportunity to teach me.

You know he wants to cut his hair, right? she says. He's just scared to tell you.

We've had this discussion before.

That may or may not be the case, I say. However, I *do* want him to keep his hair long. While my reasons might not strike you as good ones, I want to tell you what they are.

The rain starts in earnest but has yet to make the trees too heavy with water. They can, for a little longer, protect us.

Reason one, I say. His hair is like the tree in your uncle's yard, the one he wanted to chop down because it made his grass brown, which was no reason to cut down a tree, in my opinion, in the same way that strangers' failures of imagination are no reason to cut your brother's hair.

Reason two, I say. Which isn't really a reason but more a matter of interest. According to the websites I've begun to visit, because my old friend has suddenly started to believe in 9/11 conspiracies and the power of "the universe," and I want to be able to knowledgeably discuss these things with her, the bones of the forehead are porous and allow light to transmit information to the pineal gland, also known as the Third Eye. Hair, according to these websites, should be kept long, so that it can be coiled or otherwise secured, thereby keeping unobstructed the lines of communication with the universe.

My daughter smiles. She knows this old friend because she stays with us sometimes, when her husband is on silent retreats. This friend often talks to her son, who is the same age as mine, using the following sentence construction: *I love you but.* She'll say to him, *I love you but you have no idea what you're talking about.* Every time she uses this phrase, which is meant to soften a criticism—for all her New Age extravagance, she's a grounded, direct, rigorously strict-yet-adoring parent—my children hear the opposite. The love she has for her son is being slowly eroded by all the exceptions to that love. Possibly because the phrase feels heady and threatening to them, they've translated it into its most extreme form, which they say to make each other laugh:

I love you but I hate you.

Reason three, I say. Again, according to these web-sites, long hair produces calcium, phosphorus, and vita-min D, which enter the spinal fluid through the top of the brain, thereby promoting greater intelligence, heightened empathy, kindness, intuition, and the ability to sense enemies.

Your brother, I say, is very empathic and intuitive and kind, and maybe this is why.

My daughter rolls her eyes. She believes her brother's displays of basic humanity are strategic ploys to make me love him more.

She then correctly observes: Her father, who is also empathic and intuitive and kind, is bald.

The rain has stopped. Maybe the weather report was wrong. More often than not, these days, it is.

My daughter makes good points. But I have three ad-ditional reasons for keeping his hair long, none of which I share.

Reason four: I refuse the implication, made by the uncle on the island, that if I don't cut my son's hair, then his risk of being harmed is greatly increased, and so whatever future abuse he suffers is my fault and then, because he's pretty, it's also his.

Reason five: I'd recently had a dream in which I was

following my son, on my hands and knees, across a ladder pitched horizontally over an abyss, and he'd slipped, and fell, and I'd dropped to my stomach, and reached through the rungs, and caught him by the hair, and saved him.

Reason six: My students and I recently discussed what a writer could or could not imagine fictional people, who in no way resembled the writer, to feel. One of my students said, *I'm one of those people who believes there are limits to empathy.*

I'm one of those people, too. The fact is, most hours of the day, my son is not with me. He might encounter a stranger in a park and, as happened to my daughter and me, would not be believed, would actually be dismissed, if he corrected that stranger's assumptions. His hair offered him a brief chance to experience what some never do. It helped him sense the enemy, and hopefully that enemy would never be me.

The barn needs straightening. This task involves moving heavy objects from one side of the barn to the other. These objects came with the house. Technically, we bought them, but instead they feel like renters we've inherited. They have rights. As do the squirrels and mice that live and sometimes die in the walls. All have an equally valid claim over the place, and what happens in it, as we do.

One of the heavier, hard-to-move objects is a steamer trunk. The top is crisscrossed by rusted metal straps and coated with a sticky film of mouse droppings, petroleum, and dust.

But a friend is driving up tomorrow. The barn represents the type of life clutter she'll notice and judge me for, which makes her sound like a bad person, or at least a bad houseguest. She's neither. She only sees the things that I want to change about myself, and so I always follow her eye, to see where it lands.

While moving the trunk from the west wall to the south, my daughter appears. She and her friend are walking to the general store and need money.

What's in there? she asks.

For all the times I've moved the trunk back and forth, she's never noticed it before, and I've never looked inside.

The girls wedge their fingers under the lid. It's like trying to open a giant mollusk. Finally, the two halves pop apart. Yellow dust wafts out and sucks all the moisture from the air. The trunk is lined with wallpaper. The contents are sedimentary. Get-well cards for "Kate." A notebook containing what appear to be sermons, suggesting that the trunk belonged to the pastor who owned the house many decades ago. His wife, according to a neighbor, often came unhinged. One day, she ordered her husband to cut down a majestic stand of larches, leaving their house bare to the street.

Beneath the notebook are music scores for polkas and waltzes. It's tempting, maybe even accurate, to blame a place for what happens to its people. Other rash acts have occurred along our stretch of road. In the 1940s, our house had the only telephone in the neighborhood, and so became the local communication headquarters. A woman and her daughter and her daughter's baby lived across the street. One morning, the woman received a call at our house. She came over to answer it. Then she heard a noise. She ran home and found the baby safe in her high chair and her daughter dead from a self-inflicted gunshot wound. My neighbors, when they redid the kitchen sixty years later, found the bullet in the ceiling.

Beneath the music scores are two books. My daughter picks up the first—*Intensive Exercises in Shorthand Vocabulary Building*—and rolls her eyes. In the same way that I refused to learn grammar because my mother was a high school English teacher, my daughter refuses to increase her vocabulary beyond the word *vocabulary*.

This book, I say, isn't about boosting your vocabulary. It's about learning to write as many words as possible in the shortest period of time, using the least amount of effort.

You should love this book, I say.

She and her friend skim the pages of shorthand. They pause over a list of "Most-Used 100 Words." Many are "connective" words (such as "and" and "but") and pronouns except for words such as:

Day
Great
Year
Men
Other
People
War

It's hard to imagine, I say, what kind of person might consider these the most important words to know, unless they were writing a shorthand transcription of the Bible, which maybe the pastor did while composing his sermons.

I show them the other book, called *Personal and Family Survival.* Given what the pastor endured in his marriage—or what the wife did, who knows what kind of person the pastor was at home, maybe that's why the wife ordered the trees to be cut down, she wanted people to *see*—I figure it must be a self-help book. How does the *person* survive the *family?*

But the girls are bored with the trunk, which turned out to be full of anxieties, banalities, tiny disappointments that were perfectly manageable, hardly worth entombing for future owners to find. No love letters or missing-persons reports. No lockets with photos or hair. They ask for money to buy ice cream.

After they leave, I sit on a broken armchair and flip through *Personal and Family Survival.* Only then do I notice the subtitle: "Civic Defense Adult Education Course Student Manual." It's a different kind of self-help book, one published by the government. It taught people how to stay alive after a nuclear attack. The authors made the threat more manageable by breaking it into preparation categories, with checklists and forms. When faced with a world laid waste by *great men other people war,* adults could help the species survive by filling out paperwork and stockpiling supplies.

Though the manual provided architectural drawings and floor plans for shelters, and anticipated every possible menace (depression, malnutrition, delusion, boredom, believing false radio rumors that the war was over), it made one possibly fatal assumption. That the adversaries existed beyond the walls of the fallout shelter; that no unwitting representatives of the external danger existed within it. Yet the manual, if only implicitly, provided the tools to deal with such a surprise. The enemies inside, once rooted out, could be lulled by a round of Monopoly and secured with one of the many neatly coiled ropes hung on the walls, their bodies swept with the radiation dosimeter, kept in the medical kit, to determine how sick they were.

Before replacing the books and scores and get-well cards in the trunk, I sort through the layers one last time, in case there's a map. I've been looking for a particular map ever since I was told by an old boatbuilder about a ley line that reputedly runs beneath our town. This ley line explained how we'd all ended up here. We'd been drawn by the earth's electromagnetic field. Ley lines were discovered, or invented, in the 1920s by an amateur archaeologist. While walking through the English countryside and observing the footpaths that crisscrossed the hills in what looked like a meaningful pattern, he experienced a "flood of ancestral memory." The world was similarly crisscrossed by ancient trade routes and pilgrimage paths, which he believed corresponded to the underlying invisible current produced by the earth's magnetic field. The amateur archaeologist made a map of the world and the lines linking sites like Stonehenge, Chartres Cathedral, the Pyramids of Giza. These monuments, according to him, were built on top of energy hubs and connected to one another by humans responding to the electromagnetic call.

I don't find a map. I do find a tax return. In 1953, the pastor's adjusted gross income was $3,024.29. The lid falls with gloomy finality. How many decades will pass before someone opens this trunk again? Whose children will be curious enough to wedge their fingers into the seam? I push the trunk against the wall until next year. I've almost forgotten that I need to send an email with directions to my friend. She's not the sort to respond to ancestral memory and needs more practical guidance. In addition to her critical eye, she's a Cold War historian who, as a related hobby, loves the gossipy battles launched within famous literary marriages. The smell of the trunk follows me to my desk, the dust shedding from the tips of my fingers and falling into the gaps between keys. *Take a left at the house with the yellow boat in the yard. A mile later, you'll pass the turnoff to the town where famous mid-century writer couples used to live, most of whom drank too much and had ugly divorces, their misbehavior gruesomely described in the memoirs their unhappy children later wrote, a few of which will be stacked on the table next to your bed.*

Outside, I hear a loud noise. A truck drives slowly along the road. The county just finished repaving it last week. The frost heaves have been smoothed, but they'll be back. In front of the truck the road is pitch-black. Behind it appears a double yellow line. I feel like I'm watching the truck strip away the surface to reveal what someone tried to hide. I've never found any documentation to support the old boatbuilder's claim about the ley line, but if he's right, whose house did it run through? Or did it course between our house and the one across the street? Were certain people in those houses—the wife who cut down the trees, the mother who shot herself—more vulnerable to derangement by that energy? We are never deranged by energy except when we don't have it. The power around here is always going out.

The road to New England passes my father's hometown, then a depressed, half-abandoned city where, in my twenties, I did a lot of drugs with my former college roommate and her club-promoter boyfriend.

Seventy miles beyond the depot where I used to switch buses is an exit I've taken hundreds, maybe even thousands, of times in the past. Just over the river, and a mile from the highway, is the town where I went to college. Some love this college because it's resistant to change. Every reunion is an opportunity to time-travel. The same green-and-white awnings line Main Street. The same bookstore sells the same sweatshirts. The same small packs of men cross the campus green, the same stained baseball caps pulled low to hide their faces.

Many are the sons or grandsons of alumni and act as a slouchy legacy patrol. The college first accepted women in the early 1970s, but even when I was a student, fifteen years later, the older alumni, who filled the stadiums and fraternities on homecoming and carnival weekends, seemed ongoingly affronted that people like me were on campus all the time, rather than just on weekends, when young women were bused into town for parties.

I double-park and watch the students tread the diagonal paths extending from the quad's dusty center where, once a year, the college builds a tower of interlocking logs and sets it on fire. People drink too much and dance around it before returning to their rooms to cram for midterms. The tradition dates back to 1888, and like so many traditions, emerged from folly. An editorial written after the original bonfire complained that it "disturbed the slumbers of a peaceful town, destroyed some property, made the boys feel that they were being men, and in fact did no one any good."

At the bed-and-breakfast, on the north side of town, and past the fancy new food co-op, which replaced the '70s hippie one (one thing *has* changed), an unsmiling woman works the desk. Before handing me a key, she establishes the terms. There are no TVs save a communal one near the check-in desk, currently covered by a bedspread. There are no private bathrooms and no turndown service. Breakfast will not be hot and will end sharply.

I give her my credit card.

The room is under the eaves. While dressing for the funeral, I trip on my suitcase, and can't find a sock, and realize I've forgotten my phone charger, and suddenly the room is a mess. Back downstairs, the lobby is empty save for a young woman wearing a long navy coat. As I wait for the owner to reappear from behind the drape— maybe a guest left a charger in a room, or she has a spare—it occurs to me that the charger might be in my backpack, a portal through which objects come and go. A combination of timing, stealth, and chance determines whether or not I'll find what I'm looking for.

Right now, at 12:14 PM on a Friday, I find a pair of airplane headphones, a hat, and my son's favorite book, about a family of bears. This book has been missing for a week. Its reappearance compensates for the apparent loss of the charger. The backpack's universe, while entropic, strives for fairness.

The woman in the navy coat watches as I remove a pair of mittens, a sleep mask, and a ziplock bag of almonds, then run my hand repeatedly around the backpack's empty interior. Once I lost four hundred dollars in this backpack, but I refused to stop looking until the money was there.

She says, Are you Liz?

She's carrying a computer bag with my college's logo on it.

When asked if she's a student, she says, proudly, yes. She's a junior studying philosophy, and here to babysit a guest's little boy for the day.

Then she notices the bear book on the floor.

Oh! she says. I loved those books when I was a child!

I also loved those books. I loved them so much that I bought the earliest ones for my children. When I read my daughter the books—written by educators and initially meant to teach children to read—the additional lesson or message she received was the same one I'd received when I was her age. The books taught us how funny the world used to be when fathers were blustering, delusional fools and mothers were wise, stoical pragmatists who dressed like maids. Such days were so far in the past, these books reassured, that now we can find them hilarious. But the more times I read the early books to my daughter, it became less and less clear what we were laughing about or with. The mother bear, in her long-suffering silence, is celebrated as a brilliant tactician. If she stays quiet, she can save the cubs from harm, the father bear from shame, and herself from conflict. That the authors, and as a result their readers, are laughingly aware of the contorted conditions under which she can express her keenness and foresight, counts as progress; the futility of hoping that any visible change might occur counts as funny. Because while the mother bear is always morally superior and "right," she's never, not once over the course of nearly three hundred books, getting out of that maid's costume.

This might also have been the lesson that my daughter and I, when I was her age, learned from these books.

When I started to read these books to my son, however, I saw him potentially learning yet another lesson. The books prepared him to be regularly excluded from a joke where he was the butt. Women, with their angry, beleaguered faces, conspired with an audience to laugh at men and shame them with silence no matter the offense (dirty rooms, teasing, bad grades, bullies). I saw him learning that women heap disdain upon men, whom they believe to be unfailingly stubborn, silly, and wrong. Men, meanwhile, are too dumb to even notice.

The owner reappears. When asked if she has a spare charger, she pauses for nearly five seconds before saying, No.

The church is off a town square rimmed with white houses. Inside, the varnished casket gleams at a higher frequency than the nave, which is chalky and dim. One pew is "reserved for family." A certain cousin has yet to arrive. He's the one, two hundred years ago, I would have married. The woman who died—she's his aunt, and also, while much further removed, mine—would have approved of the union, even now, when cousin-marrying is less in vogue. I loved her a lot. She was bawdy, frisky, and wise. She got pregnant at eighteen while dating a man who attended my college. They wed, after which both were exiled to the married housing, a "village" of tract apartments located a mile from the campus.

Following the service, the widower leads a procession of cars to his house. People sit on couches and look at old photo albums. I hang out in the kitchen with cousin D, my husband from a prior century. We drink straight from a vodka bottle and flirt like we did when we were teenagers. My vision starts to blur and soon I can see only floating black shapes. I wish I'd brought my book because I just want to lie down and stop talking for a bit. Last night, this book taught me a new word: "confection." A confection is a collection of images that try to tell an entire story at once.

"By means of a multiplicity of image-events, confections illustrate an argument, present and enforce visual comparisons, combine the real and the imagined, and tell us yet another story."

The funeral is a confection. People hold champagne glasses while enacting present and past versions of themselves. Image-events surge around the living room. Everyone is telling stories.

After coffee and cake and sobering up, someone suggests going to a bar. Five cousins pile in a minivan. The sole female cousin, P, drives. I take my own car, because I'm leaving early in the morning and these cousins are tireless.

The cousins swarm a sticky table under a giant papier-mâché shark hung from the rafters. It's impossible to hear above the '80s music and the other patrons, all of whom sound like they're bellowing victory toasts following a war they'd expected to badly lose.

Cousin A, unlike the rest of the cousins, is single. He's a private-sphere soldier who works for a company rebuilding the countries that ours has destroyed. He admits to the table how lonely he is, and how perplexed by his nonexistent love life. He cites his redeeming qualities: cute, funny, well-traveled. Why will no woman date him?

I don't know, my not-husband-cousin, D, responds. Maybe because you're a murderer for hire?

My crush on D reignites like a blowtorch. A discussion ensues. Should lonely Cousin A request a post that didn't require so much travel? Should he shave his beard? The most reserved cousin, S, a chef, angles his mouth close to the table, as though whispering advice into one of the darkened knotholes.

The key to a successful relationship with a woman, S says, is that you have to listen to her.

His words pass, initially, as wisdom. If you want to be in a relationship with another human being, you must listen to that human being!

Then S adds, With women, you just have to shut up and let them talk.

The yelling in the bar grows earsplittingly louder. The male cousins try not to look at the only two female cousins at the table—me and S's sister, P.

P finally emerges from her sadness reverie. For most of the night, she's been silently staring overhead at the shark. She says to her brother, What do you mean? Do you think women talk a lot?

Her brother, either drunker than he appears or transformed by grief into a creature nobody recognizes, replies, You talk a lot. You talk and you don't care if anyone is listening and you don't want to hear what other people have to say.

Everyone is dumbfounded, not least because, since the funeral, P has hardly talked at all. Also, S's description of his sister doesn't match the person everyone knows. That person is an attorney who's inquisitive and curious and known for her skills at building consensus between people who despise each other.

Adding to everyone's mystification, or so I imagine: S and P grew up in what we'd always considered to be a very progressive home. Obviously, people reject where they came from. And yet, factoring out the reactionary, I tend to believe, or want to believe, because it affords me some delusion of control, that nurture is what dictates whether or not, for example, a person believes that men need to shut up and let women talk if they want a fighting chance at love. To believe otherwise is to deem nature the stronger force. Or a force at all.

D steers the conversation in a safer, nostalgic direction. Remember when so-and-so threw up in a suitcase. Remember when so-and-so jumped off a roof and kidnapped a goat.

P, meanwhile, retreats into a more complicated silence. I lean over and whisperingly offer her a ride home—one of the others could drive the cousin clown car—but she says she needs to stay. She's the designated driver. Whatever she might think of her brother in this moment, she's not willing to let him die against a tree.

I drive home alone. In bed, I read a few pages of my book. After what happened at the bar, I find poetic and reassuring this sentence: "A story is a progression of noun-verb accidents."

A breakfast of store-bought muffins is served on the television set. The cousin good-byes are unfreighted. No one seems to remember, or wish to appear to remember, what was said last night under the shark.

It's dark by the time I get home. I find a fantastic space near the city gas-and-electric van that's always parked under our windows. As usual, it chugs loudly, as though trying to digest a large animal through the hose that disappears into the nearby open manhole. I've peered into this manhole a few times. A narrow ladder leads to an underground tunnel lined with pipes and cables that invisibly grid the neighborhood.

Upstairs, the walls of the apartment register the van's vibrations and transfer them along the floorboards to my optic nerve. The living room visually sizzles. My husband wants to hear all about the funeral. When people ask me when I first knew that I was in love with him, I tell them about a call we had soon after we'd met. I'd returned from a family reunion in Wisconsin, and while he barely knew me, and certainly had no reason to be interested in my relatives, the moment he picked up the phone, he'd said, *Tell me all about it.*

However, and fuck S for throwing cynical, drunken shade at my whole relationship, what, to me, was a genuinely curious and supportive moment of connection, if seen through S's eyes, might only further prove to him that his relationship advice is sound. Was this why I fell in love with my husband, because he shut up and let me talk?

Before bed, I unload my backpack. The phone charger is at the bottom. My book is not. I send the bed-and-breakfast a quick email, asking if anyone found it, and offering to pay the postage if they send it back.

My son, who's supposed to be asleep, hears me creeping down the hallway.

Can you read to me? he asks.

It's late, I say, as I enter his room, and you have school tomorrow.

I basically say no while saying yes.

I lie next to him and grab the first two books within arm's reach. One is a bear book about the perils of watching too much TV. On the cover, the mother bear glares crossly at the father bear and their two children, who all sit, zombie-fied, in front of a television set. The other is my Greek myths book. I've kept my childhood copy all these years. I gave it to my children, but neither has shown any interest in it at all. Whatever reading habits it reveals are still only mine.

The book falls open to the illustration where Io is already a cow, and Argos, Hera's servant with the hundred eyes, is not yet dead from listening to Hermes's boring story, and Hera looms over everyone because her rage is so powerful that it transforms her into a giant.

I now know what this illustration is: a confection. An

angry Hera points, with a menacing, oversize finger, toward something or someone or someplace that the illustration does not contain, and raises a question I've never asked before:

Who is Hera mad at?

I call out to my daughter—could she please come here?—and then briefly recount to her and my son how Zeus regularly cheated on his wife, Hera, how he turned his girlfriend Io into a cow, how Hera tied the cow to a tree, how Zeus sent Hermes to kill Hera's favorite servant by telling him a story so long and dull that he closed all his eyes and died, and how Io, when she escaped, ran home to her father, who didn't recognize her until she scratched her name with her hoof in the dirt.

Then I show them the illustration.

So, I say, based on what happens in this story, who do you think Hera is mad at?

They both take turns holding the book. Confections "may contribute fresh insights, and make visible what is textually invisible, obscure, or beyond words."

Hermes, my daughter says, because he killed her favorite servant.

My son doesn't bother with a reason.

Zeus, he says.

A car pulls into the driveway. My son walks into the kitchen, filthy and sad. How was camp? I ask. He attends this camp every day for nine weeks, and his answer is usually, *Great!* My husband and I know very little about his camp, save that his friends are called Steve from Camp and Al from Camp, the director and counselors are nearly the same age as the campers, the kids spend every minute in the woods or swimming in a pond filled with snapping turtles and leeches, and on really rainy days cram into an aluminum-roofed hut, used for storing snow equipment, to watch movies.

He doesn't immediately respond.

An older boy, he finally confesses, tricked him into trading a valuable game card for a worthless one. The minute it happened he knew he'd been had. He'd appealed to the boy's sense of right and wrong, but the boy was unmoved.

He told me that I should learn from my mistake, my son says.

Interesting, I say. That boy also made a mistake that he might learn from.

How? my son asks.

Deception takes a toll, I say.

I offer to call the boy's mother—we know each other well enough to say hello in the grocery store, and exchange three minutes' worth of conversation—to ask if her son might be open to an interview.

She and I could be the jury, I say. Her son could present his side, and you could present yours, and then the jury will decide whose mistake was the one most worth learning from. Yours for being tricked, or his for tricking.

He says, panicked, Please don't.

He crawl-climbs to the second floor on his hands and feet, because the stairs are more like a ladder. My parents, when they visit, slide down the stairs on their backsides to keep from pitching forward and landing on their heads. They joke that I'm trying to kill them by making them stay upstairs, but the fact is that there's no safe place to sleep. The only other option is the outbuilding I've converted into an office, which has no running water, and the straightest possible line between the house and it leads straight over the edge of the porch.

Whenever people sleep out there, I say to them, and make them repeat back to me, especially after they've had a few drinks, *the straightest line between two points is a broken leg.*

The weight of my son's sadness presses down on the house. An outing might cheer him up, plus the tide is high and the boatyard, where we keep our new boat, is less than a mile away. Heeding my brother's warning, and not wanting my children to hate me, I bought a rowing dinghy. I thought I'd found a loophole because the dinghy, though not technically a sailboat, *could* be sailed. There was a hole in the forward thwart, into which a wooden pole could be inserted and a triangle of canvas attached. The first time I tried to sail it, I made my husband and son come along, the three of us stuffed together like mice in a sinking walnut shell, the gunwales practically level with the ocean. I didn't bother to look at a chart, and quickly ran aground, and snapped the daggerboard in half, and had to row back to the dock using the jagged remainder as an oar.

My son has since refused to go sailing with me, and only grudgingly agrees to go for rows.

The dinghies are tied up past the shed, and down the dock, and in an area enclosed on three sides, called the pen. Getting in and out of the pen is tricky because the channel is narrow, and the oars clack against the other dinghies, and it's impossible not to get caught on an outboard, but the utter absurdity of the challenge is part of the fun. The pen is always overcrowded, and there's no harbormaster, either, to grid the moorings. The town prefers to let the population govern itself, and even while tensions can arise—a person can, in theory, drop a mooring wherever they want, and some do—the refusal to hire an authority seems as driven by philosophical as libertarian impulses. The ocean floor cannot be segmented into plots and claimed, and neither can the water above it.

My son sits in the stern and conducts me between the boats. He uses his hand, turned sideways like a weathervane on a spindle. A few degrees left. Now right. Rowing lends itself to all kinds of metaphors that feel clichéd or facile but also resonantly true: The rower faces backward and cannot see where they're going. Instead, as they row toward their destination, they must perpetually contemplate where they've been. A friend of mine says rowing promotes nostalgia. It forces you to obsess over the past, rather than looking toward the future. I disagree. Rowing encourages you to use the past as a guide as you leave it behind. The trick is to aim the bow in the desired direction, and then fix a target behind you, a tree, or a house, and keep it over the center of the stern as you row. The counterintuitive motion is exhilarating and dizzying. The target, as you approach your destination, gets farther and farther away.

But I don't need to fix a target because I have a son. I follow the tips of his fingers, and trust that he won't steer me wrong. The price of a mistake is high, in the literal multi-thousands. The harbor is packed with valuable wooden boats. The yard here is famed for fixing and building them. Some are more than a hundred years old, their hull shapes and rigs reflecting evolving notions, over the decades and centuries, of how to turn wind into speed. It's like rowing through a museum. Some of the boats are rescues, sun-beaten for years in a field, whatever value they might possess too costly to regain, and eventually donated to a builder with the skills to fix them.

As we pass our neighbor's lobster boat, I suggest a game.

We must memorize, I say, in order, the name of each boat we pass. To win this game, we have to return exactly how we left.

My son isn't interested in games.

Think of it as a family survival skill, I say.

I tell him how my brother and I honed this skill when our family was fogged into a harbor for days. To escape the claustrophobia on the boat, the two of us would row to shore. The visibility was so poor, however, that we couldn't see more than twenty feet in any direction. To get to land and back, we had to plot our course one boat at a time. We had to commit the sequence to memory. One mistake and we could be lost for hours.

It's windless today and the water is smooth; it trembles like oil and briefly holds the imprint of the drips that fall from the ends of the oars and create concentric

Vs, rather than circles, like arrows pointing us forward as we move from point to point.

Vixen Dolphin Sheila-Marie Shadow Spark Annie Zephyr Scout

We repeat the entire sequence from beginning to end each time a new boat is added.

The nun at the mouth of the harbor is the turnaround point. Because we're leaving the harbor, I keep the nun to port. It marks the ledge I hit on our first sailing trip. Once our bow is pointed back toward the dock, the caution reverses. *Red right return.*

Okay, I say to my son. Pretend we can't see more than twenty feet ahead of us. Guide us home the way we came.

He realizes, then, that the sequence he's memorized must be flipped. I can see, as he works his way backward, the last of his bad mood leaching from his head.

Scout Zephyr Annie Spark Shadow

I stop rowing for a moment and let us glide. There's a boat I want to look at more closely, moored near a pile of rocks that's visible at half-tide and indicated by a pole and a neon green sign with a "3" on it, now also the platform for a gigantic osprey nest. The ospreys caw and swoop if anyone gets too close and are as effective a navigational aid as the sign. They're especially vigilant after their eggs hatch. Over the course of a summer, the furry heads extend higher and higher above the nest, which gets comically crowded, until one day the whole family is gone.

Our neighbor told me that *Second Chance* came into the harbor a few years back for repairs under a different name, and perhaps the new owner's flaunting of maritime superstition explained why he'd struck a ledge and nearly stripped the keel. This boat near the "3" ledge, at a distance, resembles it. My parents sold our boat just before I left for college, along with our house. They wanted the money to pay for my education so that I wouldn't have to go into debt. I felt so guilty that I pretended, as a joke, to be hurt. I rewrote their sacrifice as a funny story to tell. My graduating from high school prompted their first extreme act of deaccessioning; they got rid of everything associated with their recent past, including me. When, after I left home, they didn't call me for months, I knew it meant they missed me, as I hoped they knew that the story I told, making fun of how much they loved me, meant I missed them, too.

The ospreys screech as we float past them. The boat is not our boat.

Sheila-Marie Dolphin Vixen

The wind is blowing in such a way that I can position myself at the entry to the pen and let it sweep us in. I hold on to the dock while my son climbs out. I remind him as he disembarks: Keep your weight low and to the center. No quick motions. No standing. Ways to operate safely in space, in unstable conditions, these lessons have been lodged in my body since childhood, because the consequences could be dire.

I secure the dinghy to the dock with a bowline, then undo and retie it, and add a second bowline for extra security. This boat is a runaway. No matter how many knots I tie, it manages to escape and take a trip alone, but it never goes too far. Usually, I find it tucked in the cove studded by old boat cradles, resting on top of the reeds. It also enjoys finding rocks. Hitting them is an act of navigational reconnaissance. We're helping the USGS, whose survey boats sometimes troll the Reach, taking depth soundings to update the charts, because the bottom is always shifting. The dinghy and I have developed an understanding: Every day is a shakedown. Things always go wrong and that's the point of any adventure. Oarlocks sink; halyards break. We've struck every rock in the harbor by now. We've twice hit the giant, whale-shaped ledge on the backside of the island. By the end of the summer, the dinghy's bottom is scuffed and gouged, and the hull badly keyed by the outboards that grind against it in the pen. Once, when I was painting the dinghy on my lawn, and despite the future damage I knew it would incur, I tried to make the hull perfect. I wanted the boat to know how much I loved it, and so obsessed over the paint job, trying to apply the toxic, brilliant blue like a skin, without a single visible brushstroke. A boatbuilder friend came over one afternoon to observe. He found curious and delusional my commitment.

He said, scrutinizing me, You're not going to be one of *those* people, are you?

I didn't understand what kind of person he was talking about. I knew only that my answer should be no.

When my Italian employer offers three apartment options in Florence, our lives suddenly resemble the reality TV show about Americans moving temporarily to Europe for work, except that there's no question which of the three apartments is best. Clearly, it's the one on the busy piazza, where the neighborhood recycling bins are located and people party late into the night, and the dawn transfer of empty bottles, to our American ears, sounds like church bells.

I took this job not only for the opportunity to live in and get to know Florence. I also wanted our family to get to know one another again. The four of us have slid into a routine of mutual existence and logistics management. We're roommates who barely even eat together.

Unfortunately, five days after arriving, there's an emergency at home and my husband must fly back to handle it. Logistics overwhelm again, my children indistinguishable from my job, and the bottles in the morning sound like what they are: trash. But then an economics student appears to watch my children while I'm at work, and Italy again becomes a place of discovery, rather than the same exact life, minus a husband, superimposed over a different city map.

On the first weekend my husband is gone, I suggest a trip to a museum. My daughter doesn't hate museums so much anymore, and so this isn't as insulting a suggestion as it is to my son, who still hates them viciously. I promise he'll see lots of gore and lots of daggers, swords, maces, and crossbows. He doesn't own a video game console—yet—but his friends do. He's learned a lot about medieval weaponry, and as a result, so have I, because he talks about it incessantly, as though trying to hook me on his obsession, so that I might buy a console for myself, which he could then use on the rare occasion I wasn't.

We take the road that leads west out of the loud piazza. We pass what count as landmarks: the popular gelato spot, the pet store where the bunnies sleep in fluffy piles against the window, the people selling cheap, transfixing toys at the base of a cathedral.

The museum is easy to find because the noises from the crowds outside throng between the stone walls.

As promised, there's gore everywhere. I'm actually

shocked by how much blood and torture and abduction is in this museum, but at least I won't be accused of deceit, and then forced to pay reparations. I hustle us to the highlights. Botticelli's *Primavera* is miraculously free of gawkers. When my son points to Venus and says, There's Mary, I wonder if it's worth correcting him. If I do, he'll be crestfallen. He's been trying to relate to me lately on what he understands (or I understand that he understands) as "my terms." He takes it hard when he gets something wrong and I use the occasion to clarify or correct. He'd recently told me about a girl in his class, who stole a boy's glasses and hid them in a bush. The boy's friends asked her to give the glasses back and she pushed one of them and said, "You can't push me back because it's illegal to hit girls." When he finished telling me the story, he said, *That girl was sexist! She said it was illegal to hit girls!* He believed that we would share a moment of mutual outrage over the situation—girls had as much of a right to be hit as boys did—by which I understood that he wanted to cater to my interests as a way to feel close to me.

I look again at the painting. Venus, goddess of fertility, holds one hand bent backward at the wrist while a baby with wings floats over her head.

Yes, I say, that's Mary.

Because interest in the painting is already drifting—this most famous artwork has survived centuries and wars but dies within seconds before the eyes of my children—I point toward the right-hand corner of the painting, where Zephyrus, the west wind, is trying to abduct a naked woman.

My daughter asks, Why does she have a vine coming out of her mouth?

I explain how the girl, in order to escape Zephyrus, turned herself into a tree.

The tourist next to us says, Actually, that's a different myth. Daphne, in order to escape Apollo, turns herself into a tree.

I thank the tourist. I like being corrected. I expect it, because I often don't know what I'm talking about. So why didn't I correct my son? *That's not Mary, it's Venus.* Why did I think his attempt at intimacy was so fragile that I must either protect or deceive him to preserve it? I could have shown him that there are different ways to connect with people you love. You can do it while learning when you're wrong.

We leave the museum and wander toward a portico lined with statues to find a place to eat. At a distance, one statue looks like a marble fountain spewing water, then, as we move closer, the water assumes the shape of a woman in a state of rapture, reaching toward the sky while being safely held in place by a man; however, the woman, as we move even closer and her features resolve, does not look ecstatic, the woman looks terrified, and the man, as we move yet closer, is not saving her, he is restraining her, and the thick snake wrapped around the man's legs is actually a second man, trying to prevent the first man from kidnapping the woman, who, from the agonized look on *his* face, is his sister, mother, daughter, or wife.

The plaque at the base identifies the subject.

When my son asks, What's happening here? I use our expensive international data plan to look up the rape of the Sabines—I faintly recall it as the title of a painting I studied in college, one involving a shipwreck—because I don't know anything about it.

I skim a few websites and synthesize the findings.

A Roman king named Romulus took his army and invaded central Italy, I say. Since they had no immediate plans to return home, they needed wives to start families. But the men of the local Sabine tribe refused to allow their women to marry the Roman soldiers because, they calculated logically, if the Romans married their women, and the women had their children, then the Romans would become more numerous than the Sabines, and the Sabines could be defeated.

Actually, I say, they would be *self-defeated*. The Sabine women would be forced to grow their mortal foe's army in their wombs.

I glance at my son. Suddenly I'm wondering: Did he learn about the Sabines in school? This could explain why he'd recently announced to me, as we were riding the subway, *All murderers come out of women,* which I'd modified—all murderers come out of uteruses—and then asked, *Do you think that uteruses are powerful because they've produced all of the world's murderers? Or do you think uteruses are to blame for all of the murderers?* He didn't answer, because we'd reached our stop.

However, I say, rather than attacking the Sabines outright, sneaky Romulus threw a party for the god Neptune Equester, controller of seas, wind, and storms. He invited the Sabines, and when he gave the signal, his men kidnapped all the women, after which these women gave birth to their children, and then, when the children grew up—this being a very long-term military strategy— the Romans finally defeated the Sabines.

My daughter observes that the statue tells a different story without the man trying to restrain the woman, because then it was just a man on the ground grabbing the feet of somebody he loved.

Yeah, my son says, then he's just a very sad man trying to stop his girlfriend from leaving him.

There's an empty table at a café with a striped awning. Over lunch, my children play cards while I drain the rest of my data down to practically nothing. The reason the Sabine abduction was a popular theme for artists wasn't because of the story's inherent tragedy; it was not because the women were taken from their families and hidden in the woods and made to have sex with, and produce new children for, their male abductors, so that these abductors could then more handily slaughter the families they hadn't seen in over a decade, it was because the event was an example "of a battle subject in which the artist could demonstrate his skill in depicting female as well as male figures in extreme poses, with the added advantage of a sexual theme."

Back at the apartment, it's 10,000 degrees. I prefer extreme heat to air-conditioning. My husband reasonably prefers the opposite. While he's gone, I let the apartment bake. The windows funnel the hot breeze into the rooms, as well as the music of chatter and laughter and glass. I look up the famous painting *The Rape of the Sabine Women*. I'd confused it with a different painting I studied in college, *The Raft of the Medusa*. The actual Sabine painting portrays the moment just after Romulus lifts his cape and signals his men. It occurs to me that my art history professor might have been teaching us something other than French Classicism. My college's Greek life was infamous. The fraternity parties were festivals of Neptune Equester in disguise. We'd heard the rumors. We read into the unspoken reason a woman might suddenly take a semester off or transfer. Still, so much remained shrouded. Years after we'd graduated, I learned that my closest male friend had been elected, by a fraternity, as its "Inquisitor." What, I asked the person who told me, was an Inquisitor? It sounded sweetly archaic. But there was nothing sweet about the Inquisitor. The Inquisitor was responsible for sleuthing out which women had had sex with which brothers. At the weekly house meetings, the Inquisitor revealed the women's names and described the acts they'd performed or endured. The person made excuses for my old friend. He never felt that he belonged to, or had the respect of, the other brothers. When he was elected to be the Inquisitor, he felt pressured to agree. The person also promised me, as though this were my greatest concern, after learning that my friend had performatively slut-shamed women as a group warm-up to the parties the brothers threw when house meetings were over: He had never revealed anything, to the brothers, about me. While deceiving me, he'd protected me. I was meant to find solace in this.

Outside, the people rage in the piazza. Romulus's men, in the painting, lift women as if they are sacks of grain to be thrown into a ship's hold. The men wear no expressions. Their total absence of emotion could be read two ways. They have no opinion on the matter and are simply doing their jobs. Or they're stoically opposed to what's happening but must follow Romulus's orders or risk losing his respect or their heads. They might also believe themselves to be victims of the party that Romulus threw.

The next morning, data gone, I cannot load the phone map. I know my way to the university, but otherwise, despite having lived in Florence for almost two weeks, I'm constantly disoriented. When my children and I go on walks, we don't return to the apartment so much as luckily stumble upon it, and always from an unexpected direction. Before we left for Italy, a friend warned me about a condition called "mal de Florence," also known as Stendhal's syndrome, also known as hyperkulturemia and considered psychosomatic. Mal de Florence causes

rapid heartbeat, dizziness, fainting, confusion, and hal-
lucinations, brought on "when an individual is exposed
to an experience of great personal significance, particu-
larly viewing art." It's not uncommon, in Florence, after
visiting a museum, to go to the hospital. Some must take
antidepressants in order to fully recover. "I was in a sort
of ecstasy," said Stendhal, the eponymous sufferer. "Ah,
if only I could forget. I had palpitations of the heart,
what in Berlin they call 'nerves.' Life was drained from
me. I walked with a fear of falling."

My husband returns for the final week. Now our lives
can safely go to ruin. We forgo meals and subsist on
bread and gelato. Our son is allowed to buy every cheap
toy he sees and play with it until it breaks, after which
we buy him another one. On the final night, my son and
I reread, for the thirtieth time since we've arrived, the
books we brought in our suitcases, including a book
about the bear family. After a month of study, my son
spots something he's never noticed before. He sees, for
the first time (and so do I, but only after he points it out)
the smug look on the sister bear's face when her brother,
formerly insensitive to her complaints about teasing, finally gets teased himself. The sister stands in superior
silence. The brother is ashamed, humiliated. His little
bear body hunches, as though bracing for a sneak attack, or coiled and ready to spring.

I don't want to read this anymore, he says.

Why? I ask. What's wrong with the book?

Too fictiony, he says.

What do you mean, too fictiony? I ask.

Too realistic, he says.

While waiting for him to fall asleep, I also fall asleep.

When I awake at 3 AM, the windows are closed, the apartment noiseless and cold. I crawl into bed with my husband and lie on the wide mattress. In a few hours, we'll shut the door of the apartment, and when it locks behind us, the key left inside on the table per the instructions of the landlord, I'll experience the quick grief of knowing that we will never return to this place. We will never be inside these rooms again, except in our memories, and maybe not even then. My son won't remember the partying noises or finding too realistic the bear book. My husband and I rarely fight in front of our children, but when we do, I fight with silence. I could make my feelings clear with words, but then I'd have to justify my reaction, I'd have to prove the harm that can be caused by a tiny irritant, idiotically minuscule, like a dust speck, yet that dust speck is connected to other dust specks that span all of history, and once considered together become a solid thing, too heavy to move. I'd have to engage in a lengthy explanation of myself. So really, the power I assume by not talking *isn't* power so much as the right to be quiet, and via that quiet, send a message, even while the message is the wrong one, and conveys nothing of what I truly mean.

The event is in one hour. The trip to the venue takes forty-five minutes. If I can't decide what to wear very soon, the matter will be decided for me. I'm not going.

My closet is crammed to the edges with too many clothes, many of them hand-me-overs from a friend. All of the arms reach out and say, *me me me me me*. Much of what's in there I'll never put on my body again, such as the dresses I wore while pregnant. There's even the pregnancy dress of a deceased French actress in my closet. The actress's daughter sold all of her clothing online after her mother died, including the pregnancy dress her mother wore while pregnant with her. I couldn't bear the thought of that dress for sale and so I bid on it.

Having no opponents, I won.

The event is starting in fifty minutes. I try on a wool dress. Too something. I try on a flowered dress. Too something else. The event is starting in forty-six minutes. I knock over a pile of sweaters on a high shelf. I try on a dress that makes me look like my womb has been removed and slipped into a gathered sack attached to my right hip. This dress might also qualify as a pregnancy dress; a deconstructed one. This morning I saw a woman on the subway wearing a silver pregnancy dress, as though she were headed to a disco. Her friend had a small baby strapped to her chest, her finger deep in the baby's mouth.

I heard this friend say: *There's no love like a little boy's love for his mother.*

I stared at the friend's face. I felt like I'd entered a time loop. Was the woman with the baby the same pregnant woman I'd witnessed, at the restaurant that served the bird-deranging fish, being told this very same thing by *her* friend? Was I watching the literal dispersal of coded maternal lore, the kind that is always traveling, in speedy, hectic vectors, underneath everyone's feet?

Meanwhile, toward the front of the car, a third woman stared, dead-faced, toward the doors, as a boy, presumably her son, yelled at her. *Why are you so stupid*, he said.

The woman didn't respond. The boy grew defensive and panicky. *I told you it was an* accident!

The woman with the baby flicked her eyes toward this tableau that would seem to challenge her contention, then doubled down. *Boys just love their mothers differently*, she said. She might have been reassuring the dead-faced woman—don't worry, he really does love you. But it might have equally read as a criticism. *My finger is in the mouth of a boy who will never call me stupid.*

I walk into my daughter's room to get her opinion about my outfit.

She glances up from her homework.

No, she says. I hate that dress.

She's not objecting to the dress. She just doesn't like it when I'm public with my moods. What used to be a protective impulse has transformed into teen disdain, but at least she sees me, and does not look away, and this is all I want from my family. Regardless, I realize, as I walk back down the hall, and the jagged energy drains from my fingertips—there's no way I'm going out tonight—the reason I asked her, and not my son, for an opinion, is because she wears dresses hardly ever as opposed to never. Though my son and I have similar tastes in clothing, I've never asked for his opinion on an outfit.

In the living room, he's sitting on the couch with his football cards, creating dream team rosters in a notebook.

What do you think of this dress? I ask, standing in front of him.

The question makes him suspicious. More and more he'll say, whenever I ask him a question, *Is this a test?*

Sometimes it is. But not tonight. I'm genuinely seeking his opinion.

He analyzes me, as if to assess how, like his fantasy players, I'll perform in my upcoming season.

I think it is a very original dress, he says. I can see you wearing it to a party.

I put on my husband's slides and wear the dress to the lobby. I grab the mail from the post office box. There's also a package for me without a return address. I take the stairs, not the elevator. I don't watch where I'm stepping and trip on the hem of the dress. The womb catches on the railing. Bills drop through the stairwell.

The lobby floor is marble and cold. The bills stick to it. I'm on my knees prying them loose as a fellow tenant walks to the elevator, pretending he hasn't seen me. Ours isn't the friendliest building. Everyone is in competition with one another for our boss's affection, expressed in the form of a better apartment. To know your neighbors would be to risk jealousy or pity or incursion. The floor plans aren't fixed. The walls can move. Apartments invade other apartments. The insult is lasting. Our elderly neighbor, an anthropology professor, the first time we met her, mentioned an abduction that happened long before I was hired. *Your apartment stole my third bedroom.*

Back upstairs, I open the package without the return

address. Inside is the book I forgot at the bed-and-breakfast. It cleaves open to the page I'd been reading after the night at the bar with the shark. In the interim, the floor plan of the book has shifted, words abducted and replaced. "A story is a progression of noun-verb incidents." Incidents, not accidents.

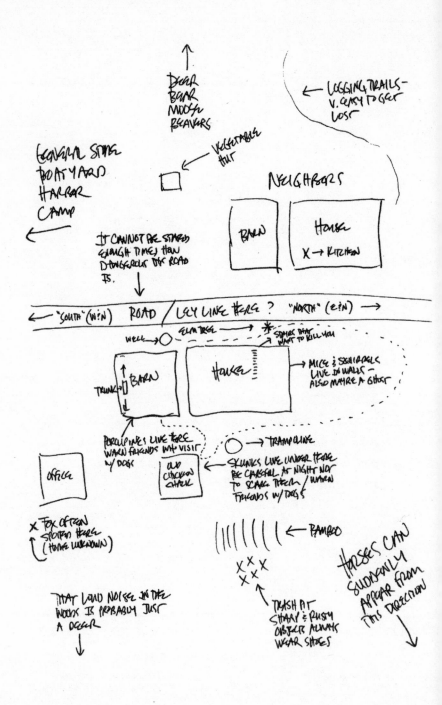

DEER
BEAR
MOOSE
BEAVERS

← LOGGING TRAILS - V. EASY TO GET LOST

VEGETABLE HUT

GENERAL STORE
BOATYARD
HARBOR
CAMP

NEIGHBORS

BARN

HOUSE
X → KITCHEN

IT CANNOT BE STRESSED ENOUGH TIMES HOW DANGEROUS THE ROAD IS.

← "SOUTH" (W?N)   ROAD / LEY LINE HERE ?   "NORTH" (E?N) →

WELL ○   ← ELM TREE →   * SOMETHING THAT WANT TO KILL YOU

TRUNK □ BARN

HOUSE

→ MICE & SQUIRRELS LIVE IN WALLS - ALSO MAYBE A GHOST

PORCUPINES LIVE HERE WARN FRIENDS WHO VISIT W/ DOGS

○ → TRAMPOLINE

OLD CHICKEN COOP

SKUNKS LIVE UNDER HERE BE CAREFUL AT NIGHT NOT TO SCARE THEM / WARN FRIENDS W/ DOGS

OFFICE

X FOX OFTEN SPOTTED HERE (HOME UNKNOWN)

|||||||| ← BAMBOO

X X X
X X

HORSES CAN SUDDENLY APPEAR FROM THIS DIRECTION

THAT LOUD NOISE IN THE WOODS IS PROBABLY JUST A DEER

TRASH PIT SHARP & RUSTY OBJECTS ALWAYS WEAR SHOES

EIGHT

The navigation in this area is chancy business. The tide runs hard and there are few bells and whistles. The landmark from the west is the brilliant light on the Cuckolds. If you come on a clump of lobster buoys, bear off to southward, stop, and listen.

Usually, the woods are emerald green and magical. Usually, the moss is soft and bouncy but there's been no rain again. It snaps like little bones underfoot.

My son and I wait in the dirt parking lot. We're going on a hike with a conversational antagonist and his daughter. The antagonist, as always, is late. Finally, he arrives. My son and I strike out for the trailhead while he searches for his daughter's sweater in his trunk and complains about the traffic at the bridge. The rangers who manage the nature preserve still print paper maps, and then camouflage them in a wooden cubby nailed to a tree. A person needs a map to the maps. While I don't need a map—I've been here a hundred times—I take one anyway, if for no other reason than to put it in a pocket to be found a year or two or ten from now, like a receipt to prove how I'd spent this day.

When the antagonist and his daughter catch up, she sprints ahead to join my son, hopping from rock to rock along the water's edge. Soon the two of them are out of sight. The antagonist tries to make small talk with me, but I know his game. He's scanning the harmless chatter for an objection. Suddenly, we hear yelling. Maybe someone fell in the water. We run ahead, prepared to perform a rescue. The tides around here are tricky and swift.

When we find our children, they're on a rock and dry.

We crouch at the rock's edge to look at the squid they've found. The squid's eye regards us with alarm. I grab a stick to free it from the seaweed. It returns and gets retangled. I free it again; it returns. I finally leave it alone to die, or calm down, or procreate, or hide.

The girl runs ahead again. The antagonist chases her and requests her, in a roundabout fashion, to wait. (*I would really like to walk beside you.*) She ignores him. In her defense, she's refusing to listen to what he's refusing to say. She's been allowed, since birth, to do whatever she likes, because her parents, following the advice of a child-rearing book, don't believe in saying the word *no* to her, which might explain why her father is so contrary with his friends, given he's forbidden, when he's with his daughter, from expressing any opposition.

As he hurries off to find his daughter, my son tells me about a new boy he met at camp.

We're LBGFFs, he says. Do you know what that means?

I hazard some guesses. Linebacker Bob Gamely Follows Frog. Lemon Beard Giant Finds Fiancé.

No, he says. Little Bit Gay Friends Forever.

He's cheerful as he says this. Possibly LBGFF is a category of affection he learned from watching the animated TV show that's become his primary source of intel about the world. Neither my husband nor I gave him permission to watch this show, and he evidently knew better than to announce to either of us that he'd discovered it before he'd seen every episode twice. When I wondered if the show might be inappropriate for an eight-year-old, he defended it by saying how much it had taught him. For example, he claimed, he'd learned from the show that it was okay to be gay. When I'd countered, *But you already knew it was okay, didn't you?* he'd replied, *I knew it was okay, but now I* understand *it's okay.* (He also learned that "America was founded on cigarettes"—not untrue—and "the first Nazi invasion was September 1, 1986.")

Still, I don't know if Little Bit Gay Friends Forever is homophobic or the opposite of homophobic or a mixture of homophobic and not.

I ask the name of his LBGFF.

He's stumped. Recently, my daughter quizzed him on my last name. He didn't know it.

I think his name is Chevy, he says. But that's not his real name. Chevy and I went into the woods and found a rock and drew a face on it and made a baby.

"Made a baby" could mean something I'm certain, in this case, it does not. I wait for him to say, *And then we threw our baby in the lake and drowned it.*

But he and Chevy didn't. They made a bed for the baby under a tree.

The beach appears and the girl emerges from the woods. She has a scrape on her cheek and dirt on her knees.

Her father, she informs us, is off looking for mushrooms.

My son throws a branch into the water. It's sucked from shore. The current, I announce, is too strong for swimming. A visit to the old house foundation, and then to the old cemetery, are activities with lower mortality rates.

I lead us back into the woods. After ten minutes and no foundation, my son complains that we're traveling in a circle. That I've been here so many times before is scrambling my sense of direction. I'm no longer trying to find my way to the old foundation; I'm trying to find my way through the memories of finding it in the past.

I reach into my pocket.

Fortunately, I say, I have a map!

My son unfolds it and frowns. The map isn't much of one. It's just a single black forking line, floating in space, with words written at the bottom. "A short walk up through the woods brings you to an intersection sign and an old field with the remains of a cellar hole. As humans come and go and change the landscape, fields turn back into forests in a predictable succession."

This modest claim, for some reason, makes me want to disagree with it. Sometimes humans do *not* come and go. Except in the case of the antagonist. He's apparently vanished forever on his mushroom quest.

Finally, we find the old foundation. About it, the map was accurate: It is the remains of a hole. Toppled rocks demarcate a vague depression filled with weeds. Nevertheless, because it's a point of historical interest, I urge them to stare at it, since there's no longer much of anything to stare into.

We retreat to the main path, and I remember that there's a field of lilies ahead, after which is the old cemetery. We thread through the hovering whiteness and enter the cemetery through a rusted gate. Among the dead: a woman suspected to be a witch, a captain who died of yellow fever, a man and his two sons, all lost at sea.

One tombstone reads, as though it were also a cause of death: *MOTHER*.

My son stops to examine the tombstones of the lost-at-sea men. When he asks if anyone looked for these men, I explain that there wasn't any point, because "lost" meant drowned.

So many people were lost at sea, I tell them, that coastal New England houses were sometimes designed around the anticipated disappearance of the men who lived in them. The roofs had little porches built on top so that the wife of a sea captain could stand up there, and look beyond the mouth of the harbor, and search for her husband's overdue ship.

The porch was called a widow's walk, I say, because a late husband was often a dead one.

Suddenly the antagonist appears. He steps between the lilies like a mythical fact-checker summoned from the woods.

"Widow's walk" is a misnomer, he says. Those porches were built so ship owners could watch their fleet returning. They were basically a way for them to check their bank accounts.

The antagonist's shirt is looped up and full of yellow mushrooms. He holds the hem away from his body because he knows how delicate the caps are, with their flounces and gills, and this makes me remember why, despite his contrariness, I like his company.

Probably a widow or two made use of those walks, I say.

That's your Gothic imagination at work, he says, as he picks a mushroom growing near a tombstone.

I wonder if you might entertain the possibility, I say, that one widow used a widow's walk, just once, in this manner.

A lot of architectural books have been written on this topic, he says, scrutinizing the mushroom before throwing it away.

By the time we leave, the sun is directly overhead. The woods are noisy with invisible insects whose pervasive, screechy hum makes the heat feel like water closing in. My son asks *how* lost a person could get at sea. What, he wonders, is the *most lost* anyone has ever been?

The antagonist responds, this time helpfully. He tells us about the oceanic pole of inaccessibility, also known as Point Nemo, located in the South Pacific, 1,670 miles from the nearest land.

When governments bring down their satellites and spaceships, the antagonist says, they crash them at Point Nemo, to make them as statistically unlikely as possible to hit anything. So, to answer your question, 1,670 miles is the most lost at sea a person could be.

Everyone says good-bye at the lot. A line of cars waits to cross the bridge back to the mainland. This bridge, though always being repaired, is never fixed. Recently, a man holding a stop sign was stationed at each end. The men take turns letting a few cars through while halting the rest. Now the risk of the bridge collapsing while a person is driving over it is either decreased—precautions are being taken—or greater than we'd ever imagined, because the men with the signs prove that the authorities know how compromised the bridge is and has been for years, and the situation is so dire that they must finally, publicly admit to it.

One benefit of the staggered crossing, however, is that we can't drive faster than 5 mph, and have more time, at the top, to enjoy the views along the Reach. To the west, which is also the south, are the islands and harbors I visited with my family decades ago. The bridge is the equivalent of a widow's walk, the visibility from the top, on clear days, fifty miles. I didn't often climb up to the widow's walk in the house where I grew up. The staircase from the attic to the roof was so nearly vertical that it felt like I was falling backward as I ascended. Why the naval captain, the one who built our house for his two daughters, thought they needed a widow's walk didn't make sense. His daughters never married. They had no captain husbands to lose (I stick by my Gothic imagination). Was it an architectural affectation? Did the father request a widow's walk so that his daughters could watch for his return? They loved him that much. Or he loved them. The house was a message from the father to his daughters. *I need you to miss me.*

We crest the peak and head downhill toward the mainland, and the view disappears behind a metal guard wall. The store just past the T intersection sells whoopie pies and cucumbers and chips and gas and soft serve.

My son and I sit at a picnic table. We eat ice cream next to a man with a gigantic dog on a leash.

I look up the coordinates of Point Nemo because I'm curious to know them.

Do you want to know the precise location of the most lost-at-sea person? I say.

But my son is distracted by the dog.

He's a real wolf, the dog's owner says. Come pet him.

48 degrees 52.6 minutes South by 123 degrees 23.6 minutes West, I say. To be as lost as possible means that you're able to be found.

My son abandons his ice cream and kneels by the jaws. Apertures of interest where I'm concerned are increasingly scarce and swiftly vanish. If I don't slip through them when they appear, they become the remains of a hole that only I remember.

As we drive back to the road that runs along the Reach, the spires of the bridge spike briefly above the trees. When we were at the top of the span, the pull I felt toward those harbors and islands was alternately imperceptible and acutely sharp. It's sometimes hard to know whose childhood I'm missing anymore, my children's or mine. The other day, I read that magnetic north is moving from its current location, on Ellesmere Island in Canada, toward Siberia at an inexplicably quick pace. Scientists recently had to issue an "emergency revision" to the World Magnetic Model. To airplanes, national security systems, all things dependent on GPS coordinates, the margin of navigational error was too great. If this rate of change continued or accelerated, many more emergency revisions would be necessary. The scientists don't know why this is happening. Likely, it signals that the earth's magnetism is flipping. In the past 20 million years, the poles have switched places one hundred times. The most recent flip happened 780,000 years ago. As the poles start their journeys up and down the globe, and when they meet at the equator, NASA scientists predict that magnetic north will be replaced by thousands of local magnetic hotspots. The northern lights will be the everywhere lights. Lights and stars and poles are like chimneys and shipwrecks. They shift, vanish, disperse. The magnetic declination from my childhood is measurable in degrees. When I was born, it was 20. Now it's 15.

The four boys arrive for a sleepover. A pair of twins, a very tall boy, a very small boy. First they play hide-and-seek throughout the apartment building, running up and down the stairs in their socks. Then they return for dinner and cake, after which they race one another to the bedroom.

Following an hour of muffled yelling and floor-shaking thumps, I intervene. The air in the tiny room is both sluggish and electrified. My son's stuffed animal lovies are no longer in the basket where they now spend most of their days. A raccoon's tail lies on the floor. Someone, probably the tall boy, given the wild look on his face, dropped the free weight on a panda. Now it resembles a giant velour anus.

My son stands on his bed with the twins. The smallest boy, who's never been on a sleepover before, sits on the floor, crying.

I don't ask why. Instead, I remove the free weight from the panda and lower the shade so that the room isn't so brightly lit by the dorm windows across the street. I order the boys to lie on the bed and the air mattress. I set up a flashlight beneath a spinning mini disco ball. Fragmented orbits of light scurry around the ceiling.

Let's pretend we're periwinkles in a tide pool, says the smallest boy.

His sweet suggestion inspires a heated debate. Periwinkles do have eyes. Periwinkles don't.

Then they fall quiet again, lulled by the rotating sparkle. I stay quiet, too, hoping they'll forget I'm there.

Minutes later, they flutter. One of them mentions a nice girl in their class. Another agrees: The girl is very nice. They talk about the other girls they know. This girl is good at four square. This girl has a pet rat. This girl is good at math. Their conversation is clumsy and ill-fitting, like their mouths are wearing clown shoes. They've seen older boys do this in TV shows, I'm guessing, but they can't generate much relevant content about crushes they don't have and sex they don't want with a gender they might not prefer. Still, they try. The tall boy says nothing. He bides his time, letting the others incriminate themselves. Then, like my contrarian friend who collects mushrooms in the woods before striding into the sunlight to correct the record—he, too, emerges from the shadows.

Girls, he announces calmly, are horrible.

The others are paralyzed—this isn't the script they thought they were following—but they quickly shift to a different script, one they also seem to have memorized, or at least are familiar with, though their tone is all wrong. They cheerfully, while still expressing affection, eviscerate the same girls they'd minutes ago praised.

Then the tall boy submits his most damning evidence to support his claim: a girl who has a crush on my son.

She's a disgusting old hag, he says.

I risk expulsion if I remind them that I'm still there, hiding in the dark, but I really want to know, and so I ask: Why is she a disgusting old hag?

The boy is thrilled to respond. Last week, he reports, the class was learning about veins. This girl, on the body outline in the science textbook, circled the area where the penis should have been.

She put his initials next to it, he says, pointing at my son. She drew a little heart.

He pauses for dramatic effect.

She's a disgusting old hag, he repeats.

Though he can't see my face, I can tell that my son is monitoring me for warning signs. In situations like this, I've increasingly become a professor whose class he didn't sign up to take. *I don't want a lecture*, he'll say.

He strategically redirects.

Tell us a scary story, he says.

He pulls on the shade, which makes a noise like a gunshot as it snaps upward. The lights from the dorm across the street fill the room again. The dorm, at night, is like a grid of many little video screens showing people reading books, and sitting at desks, and doing jumping jacks to wake up.

Though no one requested a true story, the scariest story I can think of, in this moment, is based on a true one. A few years ago, members of the university's wrestling team were expelled when someone intercepted their "locker room talk" text thread and posted screenshots online. I'd saved the screenshots on my desktop. One night, unable to sleep, I'd rearranged the texts to make a poem.

> *I swear every girl begs for the cock so hard*
> *They're all not feminist bitches*
> *(I usually disagree with the invention of time)*
> *Could see from those squinty little eyes*
> *We got a missing f___*
>
> *No Jews on Claremont*
> *They are all ugly awkward social cunts*
> *(Can I get her number?)*
> *How would I obtain a GF*
> *Looking like a dude in a wig?*
>
> *Tell him he has the tightest butthole*
> *(Nothing to be ashamed about)*

But you got your boys so you don't need hoes
At least for real I'm here now
Time is for pussies

But I can't read this poem and I can't tell them the straight facts. This lecture that my son has failed to prevent me from delivering needs to arrive in disguise.

I tell them to look out the window.

This scary story, I say, took place across the street.

I point to the lit-up dorm.

That's where the students live, I say. They're poised to achieve great things. A few years ago, however, something terrible happened to a few of them.

They failed math, says the smallest boy.

Were they murdered? asks a twin.

No, says the tall boy. They were turned into zombies.

This wasn't where I was heading, but I'm open to collaboration. I weigh the thematic usefulness of zombies.

You're exactly right, I say. They were turned into zombies. But if you saw them on the street, they looked like regular people.

So they were vampire-zombies, says my son.

Vampires can't go out in the daylight, says a twin.

And zombies are always zombies, says the other twin.

These zombies were sickened by a special mutation, I say. They could travel, undetected, among us.

How did they get sick? asks the smallest boy.

The sickness was airborne, I say. It spread rapidly

when the students were together in a room without windows and with bad ventilation. Whenever they gathered together, they turned into their zombie selves. Their sickness made them say hateful things about total strangers. They even started to say hateful things about people they loved.

That's how zombies work, says a twin. They will eat their own grandmother.

That's because they're lonely, my son says.

His favorite animated series, at the moment, is about a boy who carries his zombie sister, fitted with a mouth guard to keep her from infecting him, in a blanket-covered box.

They could ask first, says the same twin. Do you want to live forever as a dead person? Yes or no.

It's not fair, says the smallest boy. Zombies can't help being zombies.

His face warbles. His parents told me that he wasn't allowed to watch scary movies and maybe this is why. He's too sensitive to cheer for the destruction of creatures felled by terrible luck and then hunted until exterminated. Also, he's right about zombies. They're victims first, monsters second.

The point, I say, is that the students got cocky. They believed they were unable to be detected. And, so, they sick-talked to one another over text threads.

Wait, says my son. The zombies had phones?

The boys stare at one another, outraged. They're the

phoneless victims of a pact made between the parents. That zombies should have phones, and they should not, exposes the apocalyptic extent of our unreasonableness.

They did, I say, and the phones were their downfall. Someone at the school newspaper acquired the screenshots of the text threads. All of their hurtful, offensive, hateful talking, no one would have known about it. But now there was proof.

What kind of things did they say? the smallest boy asks.

They said offensive things about girls, I say, and about Black people, and Asian people, and Jewish people, and queer people.

Their school training kicks into gear. Save for the tall boy, they all attend the same school. The entire curriculum, some parents like to complain, focuses on social justice issues rather than math.

Also, each boy's family includes members of one or more of these groups.

Those zombies are racist! a twin says. We need to kill them!

The boys grab the lovies off the floor and start to throw them at the window.

But the point, I say, raising my voice to be heard, isn't to escape being caught. The point isn't to become better at hiding your zombie self. The point is to never become a zombie in the first place.

The tall boy stands in front of the window, positioning himself as the target. He wants to be struck by lovies so that he's justified in firing them back. He grabs the lovies by their floppy appendages and whips them across the room at the other boys' faces. It's no mystery how the raccoon lost its tail.

Should that have been unclear, I say. Because you can stay out of enclosed spaces with zombies. You can refuse to remain in situations where the sickness could infect you.

No one is listening to me. The enemy outside the window is completely forgotten. The enemy is inside the room again.

I shut the door to sounds of *Stop! Stop it!*

Twenty minutes later, a thunderous crash makes the plant pots chatter on the sill.

I knock on my son's door. He says, fearfully, Yeah?

The tall boy writhes on the air mattress, holding his head. He's crying but fighting it, which seems to be the greater source of his pain.

It's okay, he says, in a voice that does not sound okay.

The other boys are relieved to take him at his word. They sheepishly crowd together on the air mattress and surround the tall boy.

Are there really zombies who look like humans? the smallest boy asks.

No, I say. Zombies don't exist.

Yes they do, the tall boy says, sitting up. I can see them!

He points across the street to a pair of silhouetted heads in a high window. The other boys join him and say, *There they are!* But since the injury, they all seem less bloodthirsty, and more genuinely scared, like the little boys they still are, even the tallest one.

My son's flag football team has yet to win a game, but he's not discouraged. He wants to practice his routes. We take a ball to the rectangle of lawn beneath the building where my husband and I teach. He runs streaks, posts, slants while I play quarterback. My aim is great, but my form is terrible. The ball wobbles as it arcs through the air.

He spirals the ball back, the sharp end drilling into my chest.

He's very strong, suddenly.

You're throwing ducks, he says.

He arranges my fingers on the ball, so that the laces spin on release. He demonstrates, by mimicking my stance and throwing motion, what I'm doing wrong.

He's patient as I repeatedly fail to convert his clear instructions into better results.

My phone buzzes in my pocket. I ignore it. I'm determined to throw at least one decent spiral. Then my son sees a friend and the two of them run off to climb Alma Mater. While college students alternately honor and desecrate her, children unconditionally love her because her gown provides handholds for climbing and hides a secret owl in its folds. The owl is crammed so tightly inside Alma Mater's robes that its head is squashed, its eyes bulging and asymmetrical. It resembles the sonogram images of my children, their half-formed bodies as precious yet foreign to me as the organs that kept me alive.

My phone buzzes again. A photo of a tiny porcelain figurine, the size of a thumb and missing a head, appears on the screen.

My friend texts: *Look what I found on THE BEACH.*

She's discovered other unusual objects on this beach. The spot has acquired an oracle-like authority, though the meaning of its messages can be hard to interpret. Once she found an antique bottle shard with the word STRENGTH on it. The message seemed undeniably positive—she read it as an affirmation—until she started to wonder: Was this a warning? Was something bad about to happen to her? Would she need every ounce of fortitude she possessed to survive it?

Another time, when she and her husband were fighting a lot, she found a shard cautioning or urging her

NOT TO. Did this mean she should not give up on her marriage? Or not stay in it for one day longer?

In the case of the headless doll, my friend explains that she's reached out to her cousin, a psychic, to ask: What does this mean?

This beach is meaningful to me for an unambiguous reason: My son almost drowned there once.

But we await the psychic's answer. What is the beach telling her? I know what kind of doll my friend found, if not the message it's sending. The giant ceramic teeth I'd bought at the barn sale a few years back were not teeth. They were the legs and arms of a Victorian doll originally made in Germany. Little girls loved them. They were baked into cakes as surprises to find or used as bath time novelties. Made of bisque, they could float.

When the dolls first appeared in the States, they coincided with a popular poem called "A Corpse Going to a Ball." The poem was written in 1840 by an American humorist who'd lived in my hometown. Based on a tragic true story, this poem about a girl named Charlotte, who refuses, despite her mother's warning, to wear a coat over her pretty dress while riding in a sleigh, and dies of hypothermia before reaching the party, was meant to be amusing. It was meant to make people laugh, while sending a slightly contradictory message. Women are silly and vain. That said, you should listen to your mother.

The dolls became known as "Frozen Charlottes." They were produced in many sizes. Some were packaged in tiny metal caskets, their tops stamped with a redundant epitaph. DON'T TALK SO MUCH.

The message conveyed by finding, on the special beach, a Frozen Charlotte, headless or not, is difficult to parse.

My son and his friend have left Alma Mater. Now they're crab-crawling onto one of the two precipices that line the library steps. The drop from the far end is more than twenty feet. My attention is split between them and the photo of the headless doll. Its long dress is streaked with algae; the tides have eroded the ceramic folds. Whatever happened to it, however, might not be due entirely to the ocean. The doll might have been defiled by an angry or careless child and determined by a parent to be too disturbing to keep. Dolls are often disturbing. They draw urges from children. They may purge or predict. My mother often tells a story about a doll. Nearly every time she visits, I hear the story again. The story happened to me as well as her, which suggests that she's trying to tell me something beyond the story she's telling me. Four decades later, she's still working this story out.

When I was eight, my mother and her friend decided to take a weekend vacation together. My mother brought me; her friend brought her son. He was my age. We played together. I liked him. But he could turn scheming and violent. He'd be so calm when these shifts occurred. He plotted, waited, stalked, and struck. His parents had recently divorced. His father wasn't around much. His mother had given up trying to discipline him. Instead, she'd joined a self-help group, later outed as a cult.

We drove to my mother's friend's family's lake house, a place filled with generations' worth of possessions, including a rag doll with a porcelain head.

My mother's friend thought I might like to play with the doll. I didn't. I hated dolls. But this moment was about her, and I was being a good guest. She removed it from the cupboard and handed it to me, warning me how fragile it was, how valuable and irreplaceable.

Her son hovered in the doorway, watching.

Our mothers chatted on the couch while I sat in a chair and gripped the doll. The son darted in and out of the room, testing the perimeter. When it was time for lunch, our mothers left us alone. While they made sandwiches in the kitchen, he made his move. The doll, when it hit the stone hearth, sounded like a small bomb going off.

My son and his friend want pizza. I trail them under the scaffolding, which they no longer want to climb. Now they huddle closely, their shoulders bumping and throwing them off-balance, as they walk and talk. We sit at one of the fake wood tables, bolted to the floor beneath the signed '70s-era headshots of actors no one recognizes anymore. My friend texts with the psychic's verdict: *Symbolically it is porcelain, which speaks to how fragile life is. Also that it had no head would indicate that you need to pay attention to not lose yours.*

I'm disappointed. I could have told my friend this. Isn't a psychic supposed to see what regular people cannot? If I were her psychic, I'd at least have done my research. Objects that wash up on a beach have a past. The Frozen Charlotte's past involves two tragic families. (This would seem to matter given the friend who found the doll is a married mother of two.)

Charlotte lives with her father and mother in a remote cabin in the woods. Her father likes to dress her up and throw parties to display her to his male friends. If anyone deserves the blame for Charlotte's vanity, it's him. Her mother doesn't appear in the poem until she's warning Charlotte to wear a coat.

The author of "Corpse" was married to a radical women's rights activist. She published a series of essays called "Woman and Her Needs," as well as a book-length poem, *The Sinless Child*. Their son grew up to own a fleet of ships, was convicted by President Lincoln of trading enslaved people, and was sent to jail. Once released, he was rumored to have murdered his four daughters by overturning a small rowboat and letting them drown.

I show the boys the photo of the doll.

Creepy, my son says.

I tell him how the doll was found on the same beach where, last year, the older boy threw him off the swim float.

He puts down his slice. He and I have begun to develop a routine: I set him up to tell a story to his friends.

He and I are authors, spectators, and characters, simultaneously. I provide the opening and cede the floor. Whenever he tells this story, and to be fair, whenever I do, too, our near-tragedy is presented as a comedy.

When recounting a difficult event, we also become humorists.

He describes to his friend how this older boy—he was eighteen—threw him off the float, and when he climbed back up, the older boy threw him off again, and soon he was too tired to swim to shore, but neither could he climb onto the float to catch his breath, because he'd instantly be launched, headfirst, back into the water.

He acts out the loop he was trapped in, trudging back up the ladder, limbs flailing, then sputtering and struggling to breath. My mother acts out part of the doll story when she tells it. She doesn't explain why she left me alone with the boy. Instead, she flashes back to the time when the son straddled my brother and stuffed sand into his mouth until he couldn't breathe. His mother did nothing, so my mother—whom I've never seen, not even to this day, lose her temper—pulled the boy off, and took a handful of sand, and held it near his face, and said, *How would* you *like it?* Whenever my mother mimes the act of grabbing the boy and saying *How would* you *like it,* her face is deranged by anger that's still so fresh, though the anger has always felt misplaced to me, or not anger at all.

My son and his friend want to return to campus and throw the football around. I sit on the grass and watch them. His friend didn't ask me what I was doing while my son was almost drowning. When I tell my version of events, I describe myself drinking margaritas with my friends in a hot tub while my son is being bullied by a boy more than twice his age.

I always get laughs and, from other parents, knowing, sympathetic looks. By turning my failure into a joke, I'm confessing to my guilt. But I don't confess to all of it. The story I tell ends there. In life, it continued. A young girl found me in the hot tub and said, *your son's in trouble*. I hurried down to the beach, where my son had been rescued by a different teenage boy and brought to shore on the bow of a kayak. He staggered over the rocks. I sensed that he didn't want me to make a big deal of whatever had happened. He didn't want or need my comfort. Summoning all of my strength, I barely reacted at all. I didn't touch him save to check his pupils like a doctor and give him the okay to join his younger friends, playing in the woods.

My mother ends the doll story before it was over, too. She doesn't tell how she and her friend ran into the living room when they heard the explosion. The friend, usually so docile and distracted, grabbed her son and shook him so violently that even he looked scared. She dragged him into a bedroom and shut the door. My mother and I could hear the yelling through the uninsulated walls. While her friend grew increasingly frenzied, my mother found a broom and swept the doll's head into a dustpan. I thought, at first, that I was in trouble. When

I was older, and a parent, I started to suspect that my mother was the one who thought she'd done something wrong. She hadn't protected me from certain failure. Because the minute her friend gave me the doll, I was certain to fail to protect *it* from the son. Should she have stepped in? Maybe, but the situation was fraught. My mother, whose marriage was stable and her children untroubled, understood that her friend wanted to share a meaningful part of her family history with a child because that child couldn't be hers. Too, the friend might have been following the instructions of the self-help cult leader, and my mother was unwittingly supporting her. The leader was big on confrontation and "tough love" that bordered on abuse. He might have suggested my mother's friend take charge of her frustration by externalizing it. He might have later asked her: Did you give the doll to the little girl so that you could see somebody else fail as a mother?

My mother, when she cleaned up the mess, didn't throw the remains of the head into the lake. Instead, she slipped them into the kitchen trash. What could have been a complicated message about protection, dredged up from the lake bottom and found on a beach fifty years later, was disposed of and forgotten. And yet not. The story is about unfinished business and so it keeps resurfacing.

The reason my son and I tell the story of his almost-drowning is because we have unfinished business, too, that I hope will never be finished. I was taking a break from vigilance to laugh with my friends. He was scared and didn't need me to comfort him. I was a person and he was a person, each making our own choices and mistakes. The meaning on the beach that day was plain, yet impossible to comprehend.

The day has come. What's inside this box is the only thing that matters.

After plugging in the machine, my husband gives our son a primer about gamer culture, and how boys and men, as an acceptable, and even socially pressured, part of their patter, boisterously disrespect and verbally abuse people. He makes it clear that the virtual world he's about to enter does not reflect the values of our household, and he should be aware of maintaining that gap. Should he be overheard making misogynistic or homophobic or transphobic or racist or in any other way offensive comments, even if he doesn't know what they mean, he will be banned from playing for a week.

If you don't know what you're saying, my husband says, don't say it.

Our son knows better than to protest these conditions; this console he received, after a year of begging, might disappear before he's used it once.

He heads toward the screen, but I grab his hand and say, Please, sit for one more second.

He kneels between the molded Styrofoam inserts. They look like a cocoon shed by one of the creatures he'll spend the next hour trying to kill. Among the standards my husband and I set for him, as well as for ourselves (we're not capitulating to all of his desires): He cannot play games where the goal is to kill fake humans. He can kill only fake creatures that don't, in the real world, exist. This may not make any difference in the long term; to kill is to kill. But the killing isn't the main concern. It's the people he might meet while doing it.

I squeeze his hand harder. I'm suddenly so emotional. I feel ridiculous for making this moment charged, but I've fought viciously against this machine. Once I realized the battle was lost, I decided to view the defeat tactically: Invite the opponent into the house where it can be observed, understood, neutralized. This is common sense, or I like to think it is, because it's been my lifelong strategy. When I'm sick, I read novels about illness. When I'm sad, I watch movies where some of the characters kill themselves. When choosing which college to attend, I selected one known for its terrible treat-

ment of women. An alum had written a now-cult movie
about the college's debauched Greek life; it even included a date rape scene. That this movie was a comedy
made it even more imperative to spend four years at the
source. At this college, I reasoned, I would receive a second and arguably more valuable education. I saw it as a
worthy challenge. A game that I could learn to defeat.

My college's second education began before I was out
of high school yet. My history teacher viewed my choice
to attend this college as proof of what he'd always suspected, that I was frivolous, a fool, and so lacking in self-
regard that I'd willingly pay to be denigrated. To be fair,
when I was older I asked myself this same question.
Why did this seem to be an interesting pursuit, like, at
all? The history teacher provided the answer. Once he
knew where I was going to college, he overtly, rather
than covertly, disdained me. It's possible he just didn't
like me. But his resistance felt different. I'd found it fascinating, or I had the luxury to find it fascinating, because I didn't need his class to graduate. I was curious
about how much he seemed to disapprove of me, the
only female in the class, on a level that did not feel personal. I responded to his disdain by pretending to be lazy
and stupid. By pretending not to learn what he was
teaching me.

My son, between the Styrofoam inserts, vibrates with
anticipation, waiting for whatever is coming next. Will
he be asked to sign something? Make a blood pact? I'd
prepared a speech for this moment. I'd done my research

and found the perfect cautionary tale to tell him, about a male video game player named BigBro442, who, while playing a game in which the avatars existed as a pair of floating hands without bodies, fondled a female player's avatar, his two hands busy in the blank spaces where the breasts and vagina would otherwise be. The game's male designers, who "spent hours and hours placing every single rock," didn't once consider how certain players' virtual bodies might need protection from other players who, as a form of assault, and also humiliation, fondled their invisible virtual private parts. A female gamer wrote, in the comments thread of an article about the scandal, "DESIGN THIS SHIT OUT RIGHT NOW." Meanwhile nothing was known about BigBro442 except that he was a fourteen-year-old boy.

My son is about to levitate with anticipation. The screen pulls at him like a black hole. There are two reasons not to tell this story right now. First: He won't retain anything I say. Second: I might think my job is done when it is only beginning.

I give his hand a squeeze.

Have fun, I say.

Within seconds, he's falling out of a plane. He hits the ground running and chooses, as his opening move, to hide behind a tree so he can get his bearings. I've made my opening move, too. I've exerted control by giving it up. I match his excitement. A whole new challenge awaits.

My brother is staying with a friend two hours south. He wants me to drive down with my son for the night. Unfortunately, my phone broke, which makes finding my brother difficult, because his friend's rental house is located off many minor roads. I've broken so many phones by now that their breaking is a seasonal occurrence, like foliage or flu. One I left below the tide line. One I washed with the bed sheets. One I ran over with a car. Three fell into toilets.

The rental house, however, is on a part of the coast my family used to visit, and where my husband and I lived briefly. I want to test my memory, because it's been twenty years since I've driven down this point, and around the river, and out toward the bay, and during that time the major landmarks have vanished. The men's prison moved inland. The general store burned down.

In the end, I decide not to risk it. I dig up the state gazetteer, buried beneath a pile of years-old fashion magazines, and about as antique, these days, as a sextant. The gazetteer is the size of a large cookie sheet. It grids the state into sixty-nine segments, each one reproduced on its own giant page.

I show my son how the gazetteer works. At the bottom of Map 14, where we live, it says, "Continue on Map 8" (the adjoining grid square, where my brother will be). When my son asks why we wouldn't continue onto Map 15—why we have to flip backward six pages to see where the road at the bottom of Map 14 continues—I don't have an answer. I don't know why the designers chose to treat the state's geography like a folded blanket, or a Choose Your Own Adventure book. The fact that only page 14 is ripped and stained suggests that we haven't chosen many.

The road south heads north for twenty-five miles, then nearly due west through fancier coastal towns, the only places in the state where there's ever a traffic jam. I tell my son to look for a sharp right. We miss it and have to double back. At the bottom of the hill is a house that resembles a Victorian asylum redesigned by hippies with an aesthetic bias toward the nautical. My brother is lighting the grill in the driveway while his childhood friends crack beers and pour chips into a salad spinner, because the rental is short on bowls. I grab a beer, too, and sit at the picnic table next to men in their forties whom I still think of as little boys. My son runs off with his male cousins and their friends. They climb the roof of the bait shed and jump off into the field below. We can't see them but still hear their whoops. Sound travels on the water. The whole coastline is a whispering gallery. There are no secrets. Voices can be heard, as though piped into your ear through a speaker, over the loudest diesel engine. I once said, of a man who'd inherited his ex-wife's millions, *I guess he did all right.* I thought he was a safe enough distance away. He wasn't.

While the sausage cooks, my brother and his friends reminisce. We grew up on the same two-block stretch in large, run-down houses nobody wanted in the 1970s and '80s because they were so costly to heat. The houses had woodstoves or coal stoves to save on oil but certain rooms remained uninhabitable during the winter. We got used to it, but my brother and I tell everyone about our uncle, who often came to town on business, and who, to protest the living conditions, wore his coat indoors.

None of us have heard the boys in a while. I offer to go look for them. The long, sloping field is quiet save for the occasional beeping of bugs and birds and voles.

The boys, of course, are exactly where they're forbidden to be. The dock is rickety and weathered and twenty feet high at this tide, extending over an exposed rocky beach. One boy stands on the railing and jerks from side to side while the others cheer him on. The stick-thin pylons creak and sway.

He's stick-thin, too, and, like the dock, unexpectedly strong.

Before forcing a pause on the chaos, I take a second to assess the dynamics. My son, as his default mode, is not driven to violently break things, as the thin boy is known to do. That said, around certain boys, he behaves in a way that I understand as *not himself*. He reads the energy of the group and behaves as the group is behaving. I've tended to believe that impulsive, destructive energy, when he's swept up by it, originates elsewhere, and that he is its victim, rather than its source. But maybe the thin boy is methodical and peaceful when alone. Maybe his parents believe it's our son who inspires the violence in theirs.

The boys see me and freeze for a micro-instant, before fleeing, like a flock of spooked gulls, down the dock toward the float.

They stop at the top of the ramp.

By the time I reach them, they're still scrutinizing a wooden sign nailed to the railing.

Cyrus Chadwick was a professional mariner who sailed the globe. But he died within sight of where you are standing. He rowed off in his Sunday best and was never seen again!

The sign is the ultimate authority. It reinforces the warnings issued by the parents up the hill. *Do not go on the dock.* But the boys are suspicious. This is just another "cautionary tale" being used to control them. Who would take a row in fancy clothes? Had Cyrus just come from church? Had he had a fight with his wife? If they'd just been to church, why were they fighting? How did the writer of the sign know that Cyrus died "within sight of where you are now standing" if he was "never seen again"?

The boys charge down the ramp and onto the float. The tide rips past. The lobster buoys strain at their ropes and look like children being dragged by the hair. The boys tackle one another and windmill their arms over the edge.

But then, just as erratically, they reverse course and run back up the dock, and over the rocks, and down onto the beach.

By the time I catch up to them, they're searching for sea glass and pottery shards. The coastline is speckled with by rocks, shells, and broken items from long-dead people's kitchens.

The thin boy finds the handle to a ceramic pitcher. Someone else finds part of a plate.

What's up with all this trash, the thin boy says.

The people who lived at the tips of these isolated points of land needed a place to put their unfixable belongings, I say, one that would take them away, and hold them in storage, and return them decades later, when their trash had transformed into a discovery.

The thin boy narrows his eyes and cocks his hand, as though he's about to hurl the handle back to where it's been for half a century. He reminds me of my mother's friend's son, the one who broke the porcelain doll. He can't help but want to destroy what matters deeply to other people. There isn't necessarily a moral component to his desire; it's an impulse, or an addiction to the reaction his destruction produces. An even more generous read: The thin boy rejects inherited systems of value. This is probably what his parents would say. They believe he is, and he well might be, a genius.

Trash provides useful clues to the past, I say.

I tell them about an archaeological site located a few miles up the coast from where we're standing.

We don't want a lecture, my son says.

This isn't a lecture, I say. It's a tale of deception.

At this site, I tell them, archaeologists found old tools and fire pits and pottery shards. They used this evidence to re-create indigenous trade routes dating back to 1000 CE.

However, I say, the site was initially discovered by a pair of amateur archaeologists. They found, in addition to a shell midden, a medieval Norse coin. Some thought the coin proved that indigenous peoples had made direct or indirect contact with the explorer Leif Eriksson. Others thought the coin was a plant by a member of the Viking Hoaxers, a group that falsified evidence, such as maps drawn on rocks and annotated with bad approximations of Norse, to prove that the Vikings were the first Europeans to colonize North America.

The boys get excited. They want to play a hoax! They

look for objects on the beach to fool the adults up the hill. But the bugs, like a curtain, descend. The boys drop the pottery shards and sprint for the house.

The next morning, everyone cleans, and makes bags of trash to be taken to the dump and burned.

The smaller roads merge back into the main one like veins toward a heart. I decide to take the inland route. We pass the new prison, then the town where a famous poet was born, who later moved to a remote island, and ran around it naked, and angered the fishermen who brought her supplies, and so they would leave her for days without food. We pass an antiques store selling old bottles like the one my daughter and I found in the mud during an especially low tide. It's rare to find a fully intact bottle. She and I estimated this one to be a hundred years old. I could have put it on a shelf and used it as a bookend. Instead, I wanted it to reenter the ocean economy. It would have more value, to us and to others, if we kept it in circulation. I suggested we write a note and find a stopper and throw it back in the ocean. Then it seemed like a fun idea to pretend that the letter was as old as the bottle. We weren't intending to perpetrate a hoax; fooling people wasn't the goal, though obviously, if we proved to be really good at forgery, that could be the outcome. We soaked a piece of white paper in water and dried it in the sun. My daughter pulled it through an old typewriter. We decided that the letter should be written by a girl named Edith on August 16, 1918. Edith listed some facts about her life in her small town. She asked that whoever found the bottle should add their name to the bottom of the note, and throw the bottle into the water again, like a chain letter that used the ocean as the postal service.

After typing the letter, I'd written, in ink, the addendum "Edith" had requested. My name, my daughter's name, my phone number. I was curious how far the currents would take the bottle—to Florida? To France? We rowed to the nun at the mouth of the harbor and hurled the bottle into the Reach. We were surprised and disappointed when a stranger called five days later. He and his daughter found the bottle at the base of the bridge that was always being fixed. His daughter, he said, loved local history and here the ocean had disgorged another clue to it. Where had we found the bottle? Did Edith's description of her house match any houses near that site? He and his daughter had decided to make researching Edith their summer project.

I could have lied to him.

The father was angry. He asked me, *And what do you suggest I tell my daughter?* It seemed, at one point, that he wanted me to get into the car and drive to their house and confess to her what I'd done. Instead, I repeatedly apologized to him, and I meant it. But I also wanted to point out his role in the deception. I didn't think anyone would actually believe the letter to be real, because it was typed on a sheet of 8.5-by-11 printer paper. I'd thought, if a girl like his daughter found it, and took it to her father, the father would receive, from the letter, the message from the person who wrote it, a person, like him, who'd taken whatever trash the ocean had given them and tried to make from it a more magical day. I might have quoted to him the criticism leveled, by an actual archaeologist, at people who believe in hoaxes and other "overinterpreted archaeological finds" like the Norse coin. "The hopes outrun the evidence from the start."

I notice in the rearview: My son has fallen asleep. Suddenly, I recognize nothing. The gazetteer is useless, because where even are we on it? Which square? Then I see a familiar barn, and the entire planet snaps together. My mother eventually lost touch with her friend who'd taken us to the lake house. When, in later life, she reconnected with her, she'd called me, surprised to report: The destructive son had grown up to become a sunny, kind man. The early warnings proved completely wrong. And while the message might be that all people, over time, tend toward decency, I received this information differently. Nothing predicts anything. No outcome, good or bad, is ever guaranteed.

A cross the street, my neighbors run a chain saw. Soon, all the firewood will be stacked. The garlic is already planted in ruler-straight rows. They've built a transparent plastic hut to protect the vegetables that the deer, bears, muskrats, beavers, coyotes, and whatever else comes out of the woods at night, eat down to the nub.

The revving is a call to action. I, too, should be establishing order and planning for winter. A long, rectangular photo hanging next to the staircase is crooked. The shoes in the hallway are matched to the wrong partners. Some of the marbles are missing from a game called Nine Men's Morris.

I purchased this game at a hotel gift shop in Salt Lake

City. My family had joined me on a work assignment, and my children weren't happy about it, and because they were being bratty, I bought them only toys they didn't want. Nine Men's Morris, I'd informed them, reading the directions aloud in our room, all of us wearing hotel-branded slippers and robes like asylum patients sick of and from one another, requires strategy, rather than luck, and is an example of a "solved game." No randomness is involved, and like checkers, it can be played "perfectly."

Nobody wanted to play Nine Men's Morris, not perfectly, not at all.

A person needs eighteen marbles to play Nine Men's Morris. But I count only four. I look under and behind the books. No marbles. I look under the woodstove. No marbles. I don't want to assume my son is to blame, but he's the most obvious culprit. When he was much younger, he liked to hide things and then say, when asked what happened to the earring or house key or the passport he'd been playing with, *the wind took it.*

When he comes home from camp, and after he's had a snack, and is sitting on the couch with my phone, I casually ask, Do you know what happened to the marbles?

What marbles? he asks.

I show him the game board.

I don't know, he says.

I want to believe him. I especially want to believe him

because he often says, *Nobody in this family believes me. Nobody but Dad.*

I pretend to not hunt for the missing marbles—I'm just cleaning under the couch!—because I don't want him to conclude correctly that I don't (yet) believe him. Though he's denied it tens of times, I'm still convinced that he's the one who played with and lost the diamond engagement ring from my old marriage, kept in a little cloth box I'd shown him, because one day it was gone. I never accused my daughter, even though the box was kept on a shelf in her room. But he loves shiny objects and she doesn't. He lies about things like brushing his teeth and she doesn't.

Finding some marbles would prove that he hadn't taken them but finding no marbles would prove nothing.

I find none and prove nothing. All that's under the couch is a hair scrunchie and the plastic ziplock bag containing the Annunciation postcards. I thought I'd put them in a drawer but apparently not. Certain objects exist that are never lost and yet I am regularly finding them. They move in a slow orbit through my life.

I crack open the seal.

Do you remember these? I ask.

I show him the postcard of the little boy breaking into the house, and the one of the little boy on his knees holding the flower.

Neither jog his memory.

I know, I say. Let's play a game.

I explain the rules. The dealer will flip the postcards one by one. Each player will look at Mary's face and then, at the count of three, simultaneously say the word that describes what she's feeling.

This seems suddenly very important to assess, the degree to which he can or cannot discern, from a facial expression and body language, what Mary is feeling.

I explain the scoring.

If both of us use the same word to describe what Mary is feeling, I say, we each get a point, and if each of us uses a different word, neither of us gets a point. No one will ever win this game, but neither will anyone lose it.

I flip a postcard and reveal the first Mary face.

I say, Bored.

He says, Nothing.

I reveal the second.

I say, Long-suffering.

He says, Nothing.

I reveal the third, the fourth, the fifth, the sixth. I say, Startled, Weary, Suspicious, Pissed, and he says, more and more quietly, Nothing, Nothing, Nothing, Nothing.

I reveal the seventh.

What about her? I ask, because it's obvious that this Mary does not feel nothing.

They all feel nothing, he says.

I try to look like I feel nothing. I don't want to behave like a man my husband and I mimicked all last week.

This man—a classical composer—taught a "master class" at a nearby music school. People were invited to watch his teaching and hear music for free in a quaint, hot cabin. We sat in spindly folding chairs while the master instructed a quartet of sweaty students how to play a piece by Schubert. The master, also sweaty, interrupted them repeatedly on the first bar, and told them they needed more "content." They evidently didn't understand what he meant, because he continued to interrupt and say things like, *more content* or *imagine that you're trying to bloom but you don't quite manage it.* He grew increasingly exasperated. He said, *What are you feeling right now?* by which (I thought) he meant, *How is the music making* you *feel,* and a student said *concerned* and the master said *no,* and a student said *apprehensive* and the master said *no,* and a student said *vigilant* and the master said *no,* and then the master said, *Are you feeling how sad it is all the time, is that one of your things?* and finally, tired of language, he made the sound they could not make with their instruments: *pum pum pum PUM.* The students uncertainly raised their instruments and tried again to please the master.

From the backyard, my son and I hear the telltale groan of springs. The trampoline behind the house is our doorbell. It's how our friends announce, *I'm here.* He's thrilled for the excuse to escape. He runs out the door to greet whoever it is.

I arrange the postcards on the coffee table in a grid. While the Marys' emotions are legible to me, the

Gabriels'—these long-haired teenage maybe-boys-maybe-girls whom my son increasingly resembles—are not. Sometimes their hands reach out to touch Mary, the index finger of their other hand pressed to their lips, as if to say, *Shhhhhhh, don't tell*. Sometimes they circle overhead like a demon seeking a weakened faith crack to invade. Sometimes their hair is braided and coiled in a bun. Sometimes they're crouching with hands shielding their faces, as though preparing to be struck from above. They seem disassociated and overwhelmed, even though their task was straightforward. God told them what to say and whom to say it to. Though maybe it wasn't as simple as that. Maybe they were being tested by their master as my son was just being tested by me.

Outside I hear the sounds of springs and happy yelling. They contrast with to the stubborn, staccato exchange I had with my son, which turned the day a little gray. I collect and stack the postcards. I cannot find the ziplock bag. I secure them together with the hair scrunchie. The postcard on top depicts Gabriel, blank-faced, on his knees. He looks like my son as he said *nothing, nothing, they all feel nothing*. If the test were about the Gabriels, I probably wouldn't pass it. If asked what they were feeling, I don't know that I could say.

It's Thursday at 3 PM. I need to design a new course within the next twenty-six hours. I don't have any ideas and I don't want to teach a course I've already taught. Most are versions of *how*. How to create a fictional character. How to expand or contract time. I stare at the towers of books that protect my desk like the bollards that prevent cars from driving through the campus's main gates. Whenever an official vehicle, often carrying a prince or a president, wishes to pass, the bollards vanish into the bricks.

The tallest tower is built from books about accidents. Maybe I will teach a course about accidents in literature, or accidents in writing it. How, in either case, to survive.

At the bottom are annual reports issued by organizations—avalanche and mountain climbing and offshore sailing associations—that collect data on each death, write up the case, analyze the decisions made by the deceased before they died, and make recommendations based on a negative example. Here is how *not* to.

At the top of the tallest tower are memoirs written by survivors of mistakes. Often these books involve married couples. They belong to a genre that hasn't officially been named yet—the household adventure genre. Most were published between the 1940s and the 1980s. I purchased them at an old chicken barn that sells vintage tools. Eggbeaters. Bait boxes. Books like these. The books in the tower are designated by the Library of Congress as *1. Journeys 2. Survival after airplane accidents, shipwrecks, etc. 3. Country life—New England.* Most of these books include maps on the pastedown, extending onto the flyleaf, and they are almost always written by wives who agree to extreme lifestyle changes because (or this is the claim) otherwise their husbands, forced to endure an average existence, will spiritually perish. Their survival depends on escaping the unoriginal life that the wife supposedly prefers.

These books are gripping not only because they provide insider peeks at a marriage under extreme, outlandish duress. They are also gripping because the story is not the story. Many of the books in this genre read like letters from a wartime soldier after processing by a censor, where the wife is both soldier and censor. All threats to marital national security have been redacted. (A notable exception is *Cape Horn: One Man's Dream, One Woman's Nightmare,* written by the woman who sailed alone with her husband around the Pacific, and who states in her preface, "*Cape Horn* is not just a story about a sailing adventure. It is the story about how I, as first mate, *experienced* the voyage—how I *felt* about the Captain, the sea, the boat, the crew.")

The Library of Congress, however, is not always fooled. A novel based on the true story of a wife swept overboard in the South Pacific during a solo night watch after fighting with her bully of a husband, who is then remorseful and frantic, and in his eagerness to rescue her, falls overboard himself, and they both drown romantically together, is categorized as *1. Science fiction.*

The front door opens and shuts. My son calls out. He's home from school. He drops his bags on the floor and sits at the table. He has something important to tell me, but it's hard to hear him through a mouthful of chips.

What? I say.

A boy, he explains, did something to a girl and the girl got mad and now the boy is in the doghouse.

I don't ask which of his friends believed himself to be in the doghouse, or whether that boy or even my son was the person who used the phrase.

Instead, I ask, Do you know what a doghouse is?

It's where girls send boys when they're mad at them, he says.

Let's see if you're right, I say.

I do a quick sweep of the internet and read the findings aloud. The origins of the doghouse are unclear, though its meaning, through time, is consistent. In 1955, it was defined as "a metaphorical place where a husband was consigned by a wife when he behaved no better than a dog." More recently, online sources defined the doghouse as "where you are figuratively when you're on bad terms with your girlfriend or wife."

I choose not to share the following: "Freddy knew that if he wanted to get out of the doghouse with his bitch he'd better start wearing her thighs for earmuffs."

I wonder if *we'll* ever get a dog, my son says.

He's wanted a dog for years.

To be "*in* the doghouse," I continue, is slightly less gendered. "Somewhere you don't want to be. When one's partner was displeased with them for one or more reasons . . ."

Then the definition lapses again.

"(with the exception of a woman who could be pissed off with a man for no reason whatsoever.)"

However, I say, the website provides examples of what *might* count as a reason.

"I was in the doghouse yesterday for getting home late after work and missing the meal my wife made for us, so I bought her some flowers this morning."

Dad brings you flowers, he says. But you hardly ever make dinner.

To summarize, I say. A person is often condemned to

the doghouse without receiving a sentence or even a trial. There is no due process because when women are the doghousers, they don't need cause to convict. Sentences are typically conveyed without using any words. The cost of bail is a bunch of flowers.

He lifts the bag and pours the chip crumbs into his mouth.

Did the girl today have a reason to be mad? I ask.

The girls in my grade are always mad at the boys, he says, and nobody knows why.

Why don't you ask them, I say.

That won't work, he says. They'll get even madder. They'll say, *You don't* know?

I pick up the empty bag. I crumple it into a ball with my fist and then open my upturned palm. It blooms like a stop-motion flower.

Well, I say, handing him the flower to throw in the trash, maybe it's worth asking yourself if you should.

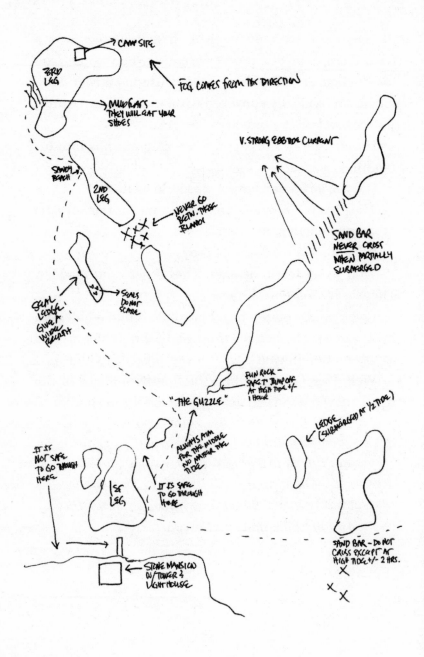

NINE

The waters here are at times the most dangerous on the Atlantic coast. Even a careful study of the chart will not reveal the dangers associated with the inside passage. The worst conditions seem to occur when the ebb strength of full-moon tide is pitted against a strong southerly breeze. On a foggy night, with the whistler sounding every 20 seconds, this is one of the most lonesome spots on the coast.

The quiet, because it so rarely happens, is a form of noise. The sound of no jackhammers. The sound of no protests and no parties. Tonight, there's also no sleep and no internet. The roaches in the walls are possibly to blame. Their hard, shiny bodies deflected the signal.

Because of the internet, I can't watch videos on my computer. Instead, I watch the dorm across the street. When my daughter was much smaller, the two of us pretended to be detectives solving crimes. I'd sit on her sill and surveil the apartment building opposite her window for suspicious activity. We never saw a murder. We did see a man whose life resembled the innards of a clock. He'd try on a coat. He'd take it off. He'd walk to the next room, disappear to the back of the apartment, reappear in the front window, try on the coat again. He'd still be spiraling through his home long after my daughter went to bed.

On nights when I can't sleep, I think of this man. His apartment is the same distance as ours from the manhole where the gas-and-electric van always parks. Something unfixable is happening in that hole, having nothing to do with utilities. Maybe the people from the van aren't city employees repairing corroded gas pipes; they're amateur archaeologists mapping a ley line that runs beneath the street and cuts through campus, periodically deranging the people above it by awakening them to the truth. Or they might be tasked with the impossible job of soldering a crack in the earth. A colleague once told me that a "hellmouth" was located at the northern edge of campus. Energy escaped through a fault line in the underlying schist and traveled along that seam, past the apartments, and through the gates. Never mind that this colleague was a Dante scholar, not a geologist. His literary sensibility was the more acute. The hellmouth, in his estimation, explained why the campus falls dormant and then violently upheaves. Even during peaceful stretches, tension hums beneath the asphalt, stone, and brick, looking for human exit points.

My virtual desktop is as disorganized as my physical one. The screen is a jumble of overlapping, untitled screenshots. The cluster near the top is the wrestler's texts. The ones near the bottom are the real estate listings for the house owned by the French actress whose pregnancy dress I won. Following her death, her house went up for sale, too. She'd lived in a coastal town near Normandy. The listing included pictures. I'd been in her kitchen, her dining room, her bedroom. The couch cushions still held the imprints of a body. The rooms look like ones I might have decorated. Pillows everywhere. Blankets everywhere. Chairs, many of them broken, everywhere. Blankets and pillows on broken chairs everywhere. It's not just my husband who hides the pillows when I go on a trip. My daughter no longer wants to live in a junk shop where there are far more chairs than there ever will be people, half are at risk of collapse, and every soft surface is covered by an itchy wool blanket that gives her a rash.

Many facile conclusions might be drawn from these interior decorating schemes. The French actress and I were the same kind of mother. An urge to protect was misunderstood. My daughter, maybe like her daughter, doesn't appreciate the excess, which is really a form of excited anticipation, for bad times and good. I keep blankets accessible because there's no telling when the heat will go out. The pillows are for sleeping—who knows how many guests will arrive and need to spend the night—and the chairs are so the dinner parties can always accommodate more.

But our daughters might experience the abundance differently. When the French actress died, her daughter sold her mother's things. She sold the dress her mother wore when she was inside her mother, which counts as selling her own clothing, too. I bet my daughter will do the same when I die. I'm not disappointed or even saddened by this inevitability. Nor will I try to talk her out of it while I'm still alive. That my daughter doesn't need wool blankets on summer days to feel adequately prepared for the distant winter, that counts as a human improvement. In so many ways, my daughter is an improvement over me. She doesn't take personally someone else's bad mood. She's polite but isn't driven to please. Despite the itchy blankets and uncomfortable chairs that might seem to reject, on the level of aesthetics, opportunities for intimacy, she doesn't consider me an enemy of affection. Even if she did, I would never wish to change her mind.

Suddenly, there's activity across the street. The fire "alarm" has gone off in the dorm. Instead of sound, there's light. The windows flash a panicky pattern, like the building is communicating in Morse code—*LEAVE NOW*—or having a seizure.

Meanwhile, sleep is getting further away. I recently stole a book from a nautical library. At one time people read these books, but now they were the equivalent of very thick wallpaper, functioning as décor and extra insulation against the winds that blew against the building, exposed to the ocean on a low-lying promontory. I performed a selective rescue. Three books. One about sailing in heavy weather, one about celestial navigation, one a personal account by a professional adventurer who'd worked as a navigator during WWII for the RAF.

While solo circumnavigating the globe in a sailboat, and just after rounding the Cape of Good Hope, he started to despair. "Another thing which I find hard to describe, even to put into words at all, was the spiritual loneliness of this empty quarter of the world. I had been used to the North Atlantic, fierce and sometimes awesome, yes, but the North Atlantic seems to have a spiritual atmosphere as if teeming with the spirits of the men who sailed and died there. Down here in the Southern Ocean it was just a great void."

Insomnia is a great void. Looking at the French actress's house adds structure to that void. The house's floor plan, drawn in pencil on graph paper, closely resembles the floor plan of our apartment. The rooms aren't exclusively destinations, but conduits to other rooms. The floor plan is a four-sided geometric shape that can, from within, be circled. The night I was in labor with my son, I walked the circle inside the rectangle probably a thousand times. Afterward, I regretted that I hadn't been carrying my phone with the tracking on. The green jagged line tracing the circle from the dining room to the hall to the kitchen to the other hall to the dining room would have glowed bright enough to burn straight through to the pain dimension I'd spiraled within for twenty-four hours.

The fire alarm stops flashing. A student stands in one of the windows that's roughly level with mine. They either refused to heed the warning or never knew about the risk. I have no boys to tell zombie stories to tonight, but even if I did, this dark shape doesn't appear threatening at all. They're looking for something beyond their dorm rooms with walls painted the same yellowish white as the faculty apartments. Maybe they're homesick. I often am. When I leave home, I'm afflicted by anguish that is not a feeling so much as a mental obsession, the compulsive topic of an inner monologue that sieves out every other thought and connects despair, and its end, to time. Two weeks until I can go home. Two days. For moments here and there, the compulsion is forgotten. When it returns, I'm buffeted by a violent gust of psychic wind that nearly knocks me over.

As confusing, and shameful, as it is to be a homesick adult, homesickness becomes its own home after a while. I know it well. But insomnia is pitted against both homesickness and home. After my daughter was born, our home, at night, became the place that sickened me. The walls and floors receded and I floated in a box I couldn't escape because the sides were too far away to check for gaps. The only way to survive it was to knock my head against the wall. *Wake up wake up wake up. So that you can finally fall asleep.* In the morning, I'd tell my husband how I'd spent the night, and I'd laugh at myself. In the daylight, the experience was so outlandish and far away, a distance measured in universes. The threat of homesickness is something I always carry inside me. The older I get, the more I understand it as love that's too big and has always been too big for one body to manage. That love is unbearable only when I'm not with the people who inspire it. The RAF navigator who sailed around the world alone had a wife and child. "What does it matter if they are not here?" he wrote. "I would not love them as I do in their absence, or at least I would not be aware of that, which seems to be what matters."

The boys cannot play video games until 5 PM. As they wait for the last few minutes of their sentence to expire, they lie on the floor and stare sulkily at the ceiling.

Then the alarm goes off and they spring to life. They load a video game, crowd the screen, and jostle for position. Ceaseless strategizing and narrating the battle in real time begins. *Do you have any bombs or anything?* I've campaigned to keep the game console in the living room, so I can monitor what's happening on it, but this means our daily life is conducted during a zombie apocalypse. *I have a crowbar in my hand.*

I read a book on the couch so I can be part of the action. Around video games, I feel excluded, even slightly hurt. *So go kill yourself.* My son plays football and basketball and board games with me, but video games he plays only with his friends. I'm left out and I hate to be left out. I'm also excluded from learning. He's gaining specific knowledge about a new world and I'm not. More and more, he quotes to me from the oral scripture spouted by gaming royalty man-boys with cartoon baby names. *A little help here?* Whenever he plays in the living room, now the virtual militarized zone, from which I could easily leave, instead I determinedly stay. As a teenager, pressing on my teeth after my braces had been tightened, ache became sustenance. As an adult I press on certain injustices that have nothing (but also something) to do with what's transpiring in my living room. I keep these outrages in a mental storage box where they're easily retrievable. Some of the incidents in the box happened to me. Some didn't. Every item in the box has been seethed over many times. To rage is a form of training. It promotes alertness and stamina but also a false sense of proactivity. *Suck my eyeballs.* Afterward, I can fool myself that I've accomplished something, just by shooting up with cortisol.

Today, I sift through the mental storage box and withdraw an assault-and-harassment trial that happened a few years back. *Nice kill, dude.* I'd met the accused man—I was briefly in a workplace situation with him—and had been warned in advance to watch out for him. He struck women when having sex with them. He harassed women on the job. While his behavior was an open secret, eventually, a woman wrote about what he'd done to her, and the media picked up her story, and then many more women shared their experiences, and his company fired him, after which he posted an online letter that claimed, "I did nothing wrong."

I'd often wondered how the man, who didn't even deny everything he'd been accused of, could believe that he'd done nothing wrong—*it's just a little sawed-off shotgun*—and so I'd tried to see the situation from his perspective. He hit women in the face during sex, true, yet while he'd held female co-workers by the hips and mimed fucking them from behind, he'd never hit those women. He might, as a result, think he was a pretty controlled and boundary-respecting person. *How do I grab stuff?* Millions of other places existed where he could be hitting or fake-fucking women but didn't. If a person were to make a behavioral pie chart, his hitting and fake-fucking of women comprised only the tiniest sliver. From this perspective, a person could argue that he barely did either of these things at all.

During the man's trial—*we're losing by quite a little*—his mother accompanied him in and out of the courtroom. His father was dead. Her face, in the photos, was scrubbed of information, as though it had signed a non-disclosure agreement presented by her son's lawyers, and so if she were wrathful or fearful or resigned or ashamed or bored, her face could not legally communicate it. *He's too depressed to be depressed.* I'd especially wanted to see her face when the many women testified against her son, but these moments weren't captured on video or film or in the courtroom sketches. I'd later learned that the son had the name of his dead father tattooed on his arm. *Oh my god I am so confused, how do you change?* What did it mean to tattoo the name of one parent on your body but not the other? Beyond a means of memorializing them? Perhaps the mother was relieved that her name wasn't tattooed on her son's body, and not just because it meant that she was still alive. She didn't want the blame or the credit for what he'd done. Death aside, if my son tattooed my husband's name but not mine on his body, I'd be hurt. *What's that noise?* I get insulted when people say my son looks like my husband and nothing like me. I perceive it as a battle I've lost. A permanent failure of my influence.

Help me, help me, don't let him kill me.

When my son's friends go home, I make him take a break. He eats a snack at the table while explaining at length which weapons he uses when, and how these choices amount to a strategy.

Then he surprises me with a pop quiz. I must rank, from weakest to strongest, the weapons.

Since I wasn't listening—my son is the least boring person, but when he talks about video games, my brain channel switches, gets no reception—*my* strategy is to refuse to accept when I'm wrong. Clearly Desert Eagle is more powerful than Hand Cannon. But is Pump really less powerful than Scar? Is Legendary really more powerful than Epic?

Epic, I say, is *definitely* more powerful than Legendary!

Do you even know what "legendary" means? he says. It means, like, legendary.

Do you even know what "epic" means? I say. It means, like, epic.

The quiz ends in a détente. I let him return to his game so I can prep for dinner. *How do you live with yourself.* This battle I failed to win, it's a minor one. I don't know that, in six months' time, when the two of us are walking home from a matinee, he'll bring up a "ridiculous" claim he learned from a video gamer, about how one in five women claim to have been raped—this number was presented mockingly by one of the cartoon baby name man-boys, and so my son also presents it mockingly to me—and I'll try to reset him without discouraging him from sharing his thoughts with me in the future, given the point isn't to make sure he realizes how wrong he is, the point is to cast doubt on the source of the "facts." I need to know the enemy, and not mistake him for my son. But before I can discredit, I need to understand why this person's opinion is so trusted. Why, if this person claimed that "epic" was stronger than "legendary," he would have been believed.

The weather report calls for winds of 10 mph, blowing from the southwest, with nighttime temperatures no lower than 50 degrees. Despite the risk of fog tomorrow, the conditions seem favorable for a survival-at-sea adventure with kids.

My friend calls and says, *We're good to go.*

When I arrive at the dock, my friend has already arranged the six kids, ages ten to twelve, and top-heavy in their life vests, on the edge of the dock for a pep talk. He tells them that this rowing trip might be the hardest thing they've ever done. Perpetual wretchedness is on the agenda. He fires them up to be miserable while I cut the fingertips off six pairs of gardening gloves. The gloves will keep their palms from blistering. Our destination is four miles away. Home, where we currently stand, is eight.

When a boy asks how long the trip will take, my friend says that distance does not respect time. He divides the trip into three legs, so that the kids can measure their progress. Instead of hours, islands.

First leg—an island. Second leg—an island. Third leg—an island.

The first survival skill the kids must learn is self-governance. They must, my friend tells them, divide into pairs, because each boat fits two people. Their decisions should not reflect individual desires or friendships. Instead, they should privilege the success of the group, where success equals everyone reaching the island alive before sunset.

That said, he cautions, this is not a race. There is no winning or losing today. There is only safety and survival. Also, we must row together. No one will be left behind.

The two girls (one is my daughter) watch the boys trash and harangue one another. My daughter and her friend want to row together, and so are being tactical. By saying nothing, they will get their way. I don't know where they learned this skill. Maybe from books about bears. Maybe from life.

After much taunting and boasting about who can outrow whom, the boys pair off. The ragtag regatta leaves the dock. My daughter's friend hasn't rowed before, but the two of them develop a rhythm before they

even leave the harbor. They glide past the boys, competing with their partners from within their own boats,
which move sideways and threaten to capsize.

I row alone in a boat that's supposed to be fast and
easy to maneuver, but none of the hardware's been oiled,
and the unleathered oars grind in the locks. My palms
are jelly before we're even halfway to the first island. To
distract myself from the pain, I plan my performance,
scheduled for tonight around the campfire. Telling stories is my only outdoor survival skill, and why I've been
invited on this trip. Ghost stories are a crowd-pleaser,
but the educational value of a ghost story, what is it,
really, except don't go into the house, don't answer the
phone, don't open the box or the door or your eyes or
your heart, don't flee through the woods or enter the
clearing, don't wear the dress or the ring or the shoes,
just don't.

The party completes the first leg. The kids run
around the island and my friend delivers a short lesson
about tides. His words bounce off the light pink boul-
ders and hopefully ricochet into a few ears. He talks
about the Rule of Twelfths, which sounds like a sinister
monarchy from a fantasy novel, and refers to the predictable math of tides, which run strongest during the
middle hours.

The tides are important to know, he says, because
they can ease or hinder our travel. Today the tide is ebb-
ing. All that water pulling out to sea will also pull our
boats toward the island.

We are not fighting the tide, he summarizes, to the four boys, who are fighting one another.

Everyone returns to the boats. We complete the second leg and land on a rare sand beach. My friend delivers a short lesson about wind speed and direction.

We're also not fighting the wind, he says. But if the weather ever turns while you're on the island, if the wind is suddenly too strong or the visibility too poor, the safest bet is to wait, many hours if necessary, until things improve.

The party completes the third and final leg. As the kids enter the protected waters of a cove, they crow about how *not* miserable they are. Their voices bounce off the water, which is flat and tight. The absence of anticipated suffering, more than reaching the island, is the real accomplishment.

The tide is dead low, the island surrounded, on all sides, by a hundred yards of mud, sharply studded with broken mussel shells that slice the bottoms of everyone's feet. The kids don't care. They haul the boats toward less soupy ground and laugh at the noises, because they think the mud sounds like farting, but I know it sounds like fucking.

They set up tents and collect wood. They struggle to make a campfire. After a dinner of hot dogs and beans, the kids wash the plates in the ocean. As the sun and the temperature drop, they get into their sleeping bags and sit around the fire and tell stories. They're my opening act and won't be hard to follow. Their stories are like the kernels in the campfire popcorn popper. They explode erratically every two minutes followed by the smell of burning.

Then it's my turn. I give them a choice: What kind of survival story do they *want* to hear? A story about people lost, and then found, at sea?

Instead, they request a story from my past, one about something horrible that almost happened to me, but didn't. They want to know how, in my life, I've survived long enough to be sitting on this island. These are the lessons they crave, not how to pitch tents and track tides.

The sky is hazy with billions of faraway stars. I've already told my daughter, and thus her friends, my most dramatic stories—the stabbed woman who ended up on the back porch, the burglar who broke into the house while my family slept and stole our car, our stereo, and a fountain pen—but one I never have.

Since this camping expedition is meant to include survival *lessons,* it would be better to know, in advance, what the lesson is. With this story, however, I don't.

Okay, I say. I have one.

The kids merge into a single lumpy blanket creature with six flame-flickered faces.

When I was nineteen, I say, I spent a winter in France. For years, I'd tried to get to France. I'd applied for youth programs and scholarships. Finally, I figured out a way. I lived with an older couple in a small town that dated back to the sixteenth century. Surrounding the town were many actual castles. But what astonished me most about France was how much, from the minute I arrived, I wanted to leave. I awoke every day in a low-grade panic. To manage it, I took long runs along a river I couldn't see, because the banks were sharply steep and high, like grassy cliffs. I liked this road because it was quiet. No houses. No cars. No people.

My daughter's friend, who lives most months in a city, mentions a combination puberty-and-street-smarts class she took at her school called Life Skills.

My teacher says you should never travel alone, she says, frowning.

That Sunday was cold and damp, I continue. Overcast but not raining. After lunch with my host parents, I put on my running shoes. A kilometer or two beyond town, I heard a car. I kept waiting for it to pass me. But it didn't.

Maybe the driver didn't want to scare you, a boy says, his fist clamped under his chin. He burned his hand while starting the campfire.

Or he was planning to run you over, says another boy. He's the one from camp who tricked my son out of a game card last year.

My daughter, I notice, is looking at me strangely: How is it that I've never told her this story before?

Then, I say, the car sped up until it was right next to me. Its speed matched mine. A man was driving. He stared at me with no expression on his face. Not mean or friendly or mad. Just . . . nothing.

Maybe you were on his property, says the burned boy.

I figured he'd never seen a jogger before, I say. People didn't jog so much, in France, in the '80s.

What's the difference between jogging and running? asks the boy from camp.

One is for losing weight, says the boy beside him, the other is for marathons.

This boy barely made the age cutoff for the trip. He's tried to compensate by offering tips. He told us, earlier, how we could save our toilet paper and wipe our butts with rocks.

Finally, I say, the man lost interest. He accelerated and drove away.

Whew, says a frequently anxious boy.

This boy hides his anxiety from his friends by saying *bro bro bro!* I can tell he's worried that I might be killed at the end of this story, even though I'm alive and right in front of him.

But then, I say, he pulled onto the shoulder just ahead of me.

Whoa, says the burned boy.

He got out of his car and walked to the middle of the road, I say. I told myself that he'd probably lost something out of his car window or was about to go for a hike in the woods. Still, I wasn't taking any chances. I turned around and started running back toward town.

That was smart, says my daughter's friend.

I really like this friend, but she's one of those people

whose compliments are indistinguishable from criticisms.

Half a minute later, I say, I heard a car door shut. I
heard an engine start. The engine grew louder and
louder until it was coming from right behind me.

What a psycho, says the boy from camp.

What did you do? asks the anxious boy.

I kept running, I say, while I considered my options.
When the man pulled up next to me, I refused to ac-
knowledge him. It was clear that he was feeding off my
fear. I denied him. I acted like he wasn't even there.

I hoped that maybe he'd get tired of toying with me, I
say, and drive away.

The kids don't respond. My daughter seems especially quiet.

Then, I say, the man sped up and passed me, and
headed back toward town.

It worked! says the anxious boy. He's relieved. The
story, he thinks, is over.

But then, I say, the man pulled over again. He got out
of his car and stood in the road.

I grab a stick and make a vertical line on the ground
to map my situation. I place three rocks along the line.

This top rock is town, I say.

This middle rock is the man.

This rock at the bottom is me.

I squiggle the river to the left and hash-mark many
trees, to represent the woods to the right.

I had only two options, I say. I could jump in the river or I could run into the woods. But it was winter. The river was freezing cold. The woods were thick and led to more woods. I figured my survival chances were better there. I could hopefully outrun the man and hide.

Did you have a compass? asks the burned boy.

You can tell where you are by looking at the sun, says the youngest boy.

But you said it was gray and always raining, says the anxious boy.

You could be lost for days and die of dehydration, says my daughter's friend.

It wasn't an ideal plan, I say.

I pause. I want them to sit a bit with my predicament. I want them to imagine me, weighing my two options, neither of them good. This is what survival often boils down to. Which bad choice do you want to make.

I was just about to run into the woods, I say, when—*suddenly*—four colorful specks appeared over the riverbank.

I place, between the man and town, another rock.

Two specks were big, and two were small, I say. Two adults and two children. A family, I assumed. They walked toward a brown car camouflaged against the trees. I couldn't believe what I was seeing. I must be dreaming! But I wasn't. I could hear the children's voices. However, I had to run past the man to reach the family. I had to run toward him to get away from him.

I use the stick to make a quick, knifelike slash. Then I circle the rock that represents the family. I circle it many times.

The family, I say, was already in the car and about to drive away by the time I reached them. They were surprised to see me. They even looked a little scared. I kept repeating, because they were the only French words I could remember, *l'homme dans la rue!*

What does that mean? the anxious boy asks.

The man in the street, says my daughter's friend.

The family saw I wasn't lying, I say. There was a man in the street.

But, I don't add, the family was hesitant, at first, to get involved.

Did the man go away? my daughter asks. She seems relieved on two counts. I escaped harm, and she is not learning a terrible secret about me in front of her friends.

Not immediately, I say. He couldn't believe what he was seeing, either. What were the chances? Finally, he turned his car around and drove into the countryside. I never ran on that road again.

The end, I say.

I lean back against a rock. The man in the street. The man in the street. Now I know why I've never told this story before. Problems resolved by sheer luck are useless, the lessons nontransferable.

The sky is still clear but the air smells like fog.

The kids start to discuss: What would they have done in my shoes if the family hadn't appeared? The boy from camp says he would have attacked the man with the sharp end of a stick. The youngest boy says that he would have vomited on himself, because people don't like to touch vomit.

My daughter's friend seems unable to imagine a scenario where the family doesn't show up to save the day. She says that her Life Skills teacher taught them that if they were being harassed or followed, they could always ask a family for help.

Families, my daughter's friend says, are reliable.

She's not wrong, but neither is she entirely right. Despite their best intentions, families are not always reliable. The French family was reliable, sort of. I sat in the backseat between the two children. The father talked to them cheerfully, as if to protect them from my distress, because once inside the car, water rolled down my face in a steady, silent stream. Did they enjoy the picnic? the father asked his children. Did they want ice cream? He didn't drive with any urgency. He didn't invite me for ice cream or offer to take me to the police or even to my house. He dropped me in the middle of town, which, because it was Sunday, was as empty as the countryside.

I notice my friend. He's lying flat on his back. Is he asleep? Did he find the story inappropriate, either because he objected to the content, or because no real lesson emerged?

I might have my answer when he interrupts the kids' discussion and asks, Does anyone know how the Big and Little Dippers got their names?

The sleeping is glorious, the night doubly quiet because of the fog. The next morning, the kids assemble breakfast in the white gloom. They haul the boats back through the mud and wait for the fog to recede so that we can start the long row home. When the fog momentarily retreats, my friend decides it's safe to make a run for it. Everyone hustles into boats. The fog removes an island and replaces it, removes the mainland and replaces it. During one siege, a boat of boys vanishes. We call out to them. We sing. They follow our voices and find us. While my friend knows what he's doing—he's an expert on this area's weather patterns, I trust him absolutely—the choice to leave, rather than wait for conditions to improve, might seem to contradict one of the biggest survival lessons of the trip. It might advocate reliance, not on patience, but on luck. But maybe I was wrong about the role that luck plays. While luck isn't a skill a person can learn, it's often credited for survival, and so shouldn't be discounted as a factor, even when it fails to appear. Maybe, too, what the kids have learned is the more important, and more widely applicable, lesson. Humans, even well-meaning ones, can pose a threat to their survival, as much as wind or fog.

Finally, the fog leaves and doesn't return.

That night, I tell my son about the trip he missed. I recount the lessons about seamanship and leadership he didn't hear, how his sister and her friend, who didn't know how to row, quickly learned, and those who did know how to row, their competency freed them up to learn other things, like how gallons of seawater, taken over the side while maniacally pumping the oars to go faster, paradoxically slows you down. I tell him about the Big and Little Dipper, both parts of bigger constellations called Ursa Major and Ursa Minor, and how a mother was turned into a bear because Zeus was unfaithful to his wife, and when the mother's son mistook her for a mortal threat and tried to kill her, Zeus turned him into a bear, too.

That guy likes to turn people into animals, he says.

He does, I say. However, because the mother and the son were bears, and Zeus felt bad for them, and yet for some reason their transformations couldn't be reversed, he grabbed them by the tails and threw them into the night sky, where they could live for eternity. Which is both a happy ending and a sad one.

Why sad? he asks.

Because they'll be together forever, I say. But their paws can never touch.

I feel around the blankets for his hand to underscore that sadness. Some nights—fewer and fewer, but still, some—he asks me to stay in his bed until he's asleep.

Tonight, maybe because he missed me, he asks me to stay. I really need to get some work done, but I hold his hand and lie beside him and wait for the involuntary jerking that means he's dropping toward a dream. He's lectured me in the past about leaving when I think he's asleep but he's not. Rather than sneaking out, as I did when he was a baby, a toddler, even a six-year-old child, he says, he'd prefer me to be direct. He wants to know if I'm leaving. He's old enough to handle it.

But I'm not old enough to accept that my presence isn't absolutely essential for him to feel safe enough to fall and stay asleep.

When he's breathing evenly, his head toward the bookcase, I slide my legs over the side of the bed and hang on my heels. Then I stand up and creep toward the door, and turn to check on him just before I slip around the jamb.

His arm reaches out to pat the mattress where my body should have been.

When he speaks, his voice is neutral and patient, as it is when he's trying to coach me to throw a better spiral, stronger and more direct.

Please just tell me if you're leaving, he says. I don't want to reach for air.

I drive at 80 mph and outperform the phone map predictions by thirty minutes. I pass the oil tanks and the scrap iron heap and cross what was once a familiar bridge with its view of the airport. But the right exit is suddenly the wrong, and I'm looping, via a narrow road, onto an island with a hospital. Who built a hospital on an island? Furthermore, where did this island come from?

A road behind the hospital leads back to the mainland, and joins the one that passes the strip mall, failing now for fifty years, and named after the historic train station the city razed to build it. Whenever I visit my hometown, or briefly pass through on my way north or south, I drive past my old house. I have no idea who bought it when my family sold it. I have no idea how many owners it's had since we left. Recently the house came up for sale again, and the famous writer who equated one baby with one book considered buying it. He'd mentioned this to me, in passing, at a work function, because now he's my colleague and can't as easily pretend not to know me. My reaction was immediate and ferocious. I wanted to say to him, *I forbid it.* Instead, I told him how impossible the house was to heat and maintain. It was needier than ten children. If he bought the house, I implied, he'd never write another book.

The road curves along the perimeter of the cemetery, now a kempt-looking park where people in quilted vests walk their dogs. From below, my old house is even more exposed than usual on top of the hill. The house was originally designed with two turrets, one north and one south. Only the south turret existed by the time we moved in. At some point, after the naval man's daughters died, a person bought the north side of the house and removed the turret and enlarged the floor plan so that the living room extended to the edge of the lawn. The north side had a dumbwaiter and nine bathrooms and a squash court in the attic. The south side, where we lived, had no dumbwaiter and one bathroom. Instead of a squash court, our attic had trunks of the father's old naval uniforms and a Victrola missing its horn. We also had harmony and the north side did not. The north side was so big, or so cursed, most of the families lasted barely three years before the parents decided to divorce, and sell the house to another family, with parents who would soon divorce, and on it went. We were constantly having to befriend new children so that we'd be allowed through the door in the attic, the only connection between the two sides, to play dodgeball in the squash court during the winter, when it was too cold to be outside.

Three blocks later I arrive at my friend's house, which used to be a different friend's house forty years ago.

She suggests a walk before dinner. She says, Let's go by your old house! I tell her that I already did, but she insists. When we reach the driveway, I understand why the house appears so unprotected. The wooden fence is gone and so are the stubby evergreen bushes. Everything's been cropped away. An SUV fills the driveway. A man rides a pristine backhoe around the tiny backyard. My friend grabs my arm, dragging me up the drive. I realize, now: I'm her excuse to meet these people. He and his wife are new to the neighborhood.

The man pretends not to notice the strangers on his property. My friend is undaunted. She yells, as though unveiling a surprise, She grew up in this house!

He kills the engine and dismounts. He doesn't introduce himself or even look at me. Instead, he gazes toward the house's roofline. He talks about how expensive it was to replace the vinyl siding, and then lists everything that used to be wrong with the house but now, because he's fixed it, isn't.

The man's wife emerges from a side door and walks

down the steps where, decades earlier, the bloody nylon stocking was discovered. My friend introduces me again, with the same expectant fanfare, which is met with the same suspicious disinterest. The wife talks about how they've converted the third floor into an office suite, and numbers the bathrooms they've added. She acts like the house barely had plumbing when they arrived, and to be fair, when my family lived there, it had only the one bathroom, and no shower, just a tub. On weekday mornings, my mother took a bath, and then I did, and then my brother did, all in the same water, because the heater couldn't manage more than two hot baths, and then the tub was drained and refilled for my father. This situation never seemed odd until a friend, in high school, stayed with me for a week. Because she was the guest, she got the first bath. I had to teach her how to wash her hair in a tub. The first time she tried it, she cried. I sat on the clothes hamper to talk her through her panic, her hair fanned out in the soapy water, her desperate fingers scrubbing.

When the wife invites us inside, my friend says, Great! and I say, No, thank you.

At the restaurant, the drinks arrive immediately. My friend apologizes for taking me to the house.

I'd heard those people weren't very nice, she says.

We order two rounds of drinks and soon I have to pee. The restroom is located at the end of a hallway. A man and a woman stand in line, talking.

MAN: He ended up on top of her.

WOMAN: Wow.

MAN: It happened in music class. He says he was walking across the classroom and he "ended up on top of her."

WOMAN: Okay.

MAN: And then he said she attacked him and so he had to pull her hair in self-defense. He told the kindergarten teacher that he "didn't know that girls' hair hurt."

WOMAN: [Laughs uncomfortably] Right.

MAN: It all sounds pretty fishy.

WOMAN: Would it have made a difference if he'd pulled a boy's hair?

MAN: Definitely. This is way worse.

WOMAN: Huh.

MAN: He knows he's so busted. He needs to get his story straight.

WOMAN: Yeah.

MAN: I told him we have to get on the same page about this.

WOMAN: Definitely.

A person exits the restroom and the man goes in. The woman and I stand alone in the hall. She's younger than the man. I consider asking if by saying *okay, right, huh, yeah, definitely* she was agreeing with him, or politely opting out of learning something about him she'd rather not know. Why was it worse that his son (the boy is clearly his son) attacked a girl, rather than a boy? I wanted to know both why she asked that question and what she'd made of his answer.

Back at the table, I tell my friend what I overheard. I point out the man and the woman, now sitting at the bar, their heads nearly touching.

Get his story straight! she says.

She works in PR for a bank. She's their preemptive fixer. Her job is to iron all the kinks from the bank's stories before she gives them to the media.

They're sleeping together, she says. He's married. She's not.

Who cares, I say. I'm more interested in what the man said to her in the hallway. It seems connected to something that happened at our dinner table a few nights ago. My daughter mentioned a girl in her class that nobody liked, and my son said, *Maybe that's because she's too much of a feminist.*

I'm pretty sure, I say, that my son was repeating something he'd heard from one of the gamers he follows, and so I demonstrated what would happen if we took his statement "too much of a feminist" to its logical conclusion. To be called "too much of a feminist" suggested that a person could believe *too much* in gender equality. In order to not believe too much in equality, a person had to believe in it less. To believe less in equality meant that you needed, in order to believe in equality in the exact right amount, to not believe in equality.

My friend winks and lifts her glass.

Cheers to that, she says.

The man and woman get up from their stools. He helps her with her coat. He guides her by the waist through the happy-hour throng, and this, added to what I overheard earlier, doesn't eliminate the possibility that he's cheating on somebody to be with her, but, if so, he's not worried about being caught. It's clear from the way he maneuvers the woman, who is shyly beautiful, that his association with her makes him proud, and worth whatever risk to show it off. If his partner finds out he's not working late or at the gym, he'll just have to get his story straight, and presumably this won't be a problem. He's had a lot of practice, and so, someday, will his son.

My friend orders dessert and then goes to the restroom. Through the window, the man and the woman face each other on the sidewalk. Suddenly, the woman rushes off. The man's posture slumps. He lights a cigarette and leans against a parking meter. Now I feel guilty. I've inhabited him like the people who bought my old house and assumed the vinyl siding was a sign of disrepair, rather than the best available option to protect it. He's probably a lonely divorcé who's finally, after years alone, fallen in love with someone who doesn't love him back, and maybe, too, when he said, *He needs to get his story straight,* he was announcing to his son, *You've got to stop lying and get on the same page, with me, your father, who tolerates no disrespect to women of any age.*

Because it's almost ten, I text my daughter before she

goes to bed, to tell her how blue it made me to see my old house. I tell her how worried I am that our current house might someday be inhabited by mean people.

She doesn't respond. Out the back window of the restaurant is my old elementary school, a brutalist brick-and-concrete bunker, built in the mid-'70s to replace the Victorian one with the high ceilings and exorbitant heating bill, later converted into condominiums. The new school reflected progressive ideas about child education, and so the floor plan was designed without any interior walls. The teachers used low bookshelves and chalkboards on wheels to draw and redraw the "classrooms" on the industrial carpet. Then the school system decided in the '90s: Children needed walls.

My friend is still in line for the bathroom. She's probably deep in conversation with a stranger. She likes talking to strangers, plus the hallway is designed so that the people waiting in it can't help but interact. Once I went to a thermal spa in the Swiss Alps, also brutalist and visually forbidding yet designed in such a way that I found myself uttering in overheated amazement, *This is a building made for people.* Sometimes people are the buildings as well as the inhabitants. I have been a building. Twice in my life, while pregnant, my body hosted tenants. Now the situation is reversed. I'm the temporary guest in my children's bodies. I inhabit them with my ideas, my language, my intonation. I hear myself talking when they talk. This can be alarming, like when my former students come to my office and say, *I've never forgotten what you said about X,* and when they repeat back to me what I told them about X, not only do I not remember saying what I apparently said, but I also can't imagine any part of me ever believing such a statement to be true because I wholeheartedly disagree with it. More terrifying is the likelihood that this "wisdom" has been passed along, replicating indefinitely, with my endorsement.

Finally, my daughter texts me back.

Just don't sell it to jerks.

On the way back to my friend's house, we walk past the school, brightly lit as though a film is being shot while the now-rooms are empty of children. I wasn't really asking my daughter for her advice. I was testing to see if she'd say, *You don't need to worry because you will own it until you die and then we will never sell it.* If she doesn't love this house as much as I do does that mean she doesn't love her childhood as much as I do? But houses aren't photo albums. Houses can't be stashed in the attic of another house. They need to reenter the economy like all the objects they contain so that they'll maintain their worth and never be forgotten. When I first moved to the city in my twenties, I lived across an industrial street from a factory that stayed lit throughout the night. I could sit in the window and watch the machines running. My mother, after she visited me for the first time, framed a famous poem titled after the street. The poem, or so we were told, referred to the very factory that I could see through my windows. I memorized the line that concluded each stanza. I heard it in my head whenever I watched the machines, their reassuring, visual rhythm like a second heart beating below mine. *And I shall sell you, sell you, of course, my dear, and you'll sell me.* Some interpreted the line as cynical, bleak; "trapped in a relationship of consumerism," according to one critic. I saw it as a hopeful reminder of how love can change hands and still thrive. Value is not solely to be had in the keeping.

At the apartment, our brief absence can be measured. We were gone and trees flowered. We were gone and my son has done none of his vacation homework. Together, we look at the assignments. The first: He must read an entire book. The second: He must write, in the form of a diary, and based on the research he'd collected, the experience of a boy crossing the Atlantic on the *Mayflower*.

He sits at my computer and types out a diary entry.

We got to the ship. Someone on deck said, "That bucket is your bathroom." Our whole family said "WHAT!" Except my mother. She said, "We have to survive." I am getting annoyed because my mother is not helping and she keeps saying, "Deal with it." I'm kind of fed up. But my father is helping a lot and I am really grateful. There was a warning of a horrible storm and it hit. My responsibility has risen because I have to take care of my younger sister, my younger brother, and me! But my mother still isn't helping anybody! Now I know that anything bad could happen.

I have a question, I say. Why is the mother portrayed as such a heartless person?

Even as I say this, I'm realizing that *I* don't think she's a heartless person. She is a smart, realistic, efficient person. The question should have been, *Why does her son find her heartless when she's just asking people to take responsibility, work together, and accept change, so that everyone can stay alive?*

That's what the article said, he says.

For the second time ever in his life, I'm wondering if I need to contact his school. Earlier in the year, he'd written a research paper about acupuncture. "Yin is happy, nice fun and male," he'd written, "and yang is mean depressed negative and female." I sent an email to his teacher wondering what websites or magazines he might be reading. The teacher responded, *As we look to revise these pieces during the coming few days, I will certainly take a look at the articles he referenced and see what type of interpretation he had of the text.*

It's difficult to imagine, I say, what sort of article

would describe a mother's behavior on the *Mayflower*. Certainly, there were more pressing details to commit to history.

He shrugs. Well, he says, that's just what I read somewhere.

I ask him to find the book he was supposed to finish before school started again.

He's read zero pages.

It's boring, he says.

I offer him a deal. I'll buy him the fake designer scarf he's been begging for if he promises to choose another book—any book—off the shelf to read "for pleasure."

I fully understand, I say, that it's impossible to command a person to experience pleasure. The point is to read a book not assigned in school. You can totally hate the book you're reading for pleasure, and I will still buy you a scarf.

He considers the deal.

But there's some fine print, I say. You must not only finish the book within one week, but you must also report what happens in each chapter, and make predictions about the plot. What does the hole in the tree portend? What does the talking horse portend?

If a person can see the future in books, I say, they'll be better able to see the future in life, too.

He really wants this scarf. But first he wants to challenge the premise of my bribe.

Why are adults so obsessed with the future? he says.

Because it's optimistic, I say. The future is something

to dream about. How might the future be better than the present? Also, it's good strategy. A person doesn't want to end up in a bad future that might have been avoided.

Whenever I do something wrong in school, he says, my teachers tell me, *In the future, you should ask first. In the future, you should share the markers. In the future, you should remember a raincoat.*

If they want me to change right now, he says, it's not very smart.

Why not? I ask.

Because whenever they tell me to think about the future, he says, I imagine myself as an old man finally remembering my raincoat.

He chooses a book from the shelf. I grab my book, too, and sit on the couch beside him. Peripherally, I watch him read the outside of his book, not the inside.

You need to start reading your book, I say, or it will take you until the next century to finish it, and you won't earn the scarf.

Unless I get cancer, he says, I will still be alive in the next century. So that's not a problem.

But I won't be alive in the next century, I say, and my will won't say anything about owing anyone a scarf.

You could be immortal, he says.

Despite being very competitive, I tell him, even against undefeated opponents like time and death, I'm probably not immortal, but hopefully I won't be able to confirm this for a few more decades. I do, however, want to live to be the oldest person in the world. I want to break a record, not in my life but with it. A life is the most valuable item I possess.

If I really cared about your ability to see the future, I say, I should have traded my life for you to read the book you're still not reading.

He opens the book.

Five minutes later, he's still on the first page.

I don't want to be immortal, he says.

Why? I ask.

If I were immortal, he says, I'd have to keep making new friends. Also, a person would have to keep learning different ways of being alive.

What do you mean? I ask.

One century you're walking on two legs, he says, and the next century you're riding a hover board.

He returns his eyes to the book.

That would be hard, he says. If the world completely changed, and you had to keep changing, too.

It's Saturday night. The temperature has dropped. I root around my pocket for a hair elastic and find a grocery receipt. The back is filled with notes in my handwriting that I don't remember taking.

> *Hovering about the landscape of fields*
> *Pilots make letters in the world so*
> *The pilots could see.*
> *Swimming pools and parking lots*
> *Speed and ribbon*
> *Smashing literature into landscape*
> *Childhood can seem like a crime scene.*

The pedestrian signal is a red hand. I'm not going anywhere—I'm just roaming the blocks like the campus security guards—and so patiently wait for the light to turn. The neighborhood is demarcated, to the east and west, by cliffs. It's far less dangerous than it used to be, though occasionally the university "community" receives an email from an administrator named Michael alerting us to a local crime, typically a mugging or a lobby package theft. Victims and perps fall into one of two categories: "affiliates" and "nonaffiliates." Michael prefers language that's detached, depersonalized, and certain. The nonaffiliate "did enter using an unknown device to manipulate the lock" and "did rip open three packages and remove their contents" and "did approach the affiliate from behind" and "did demand his moped."

His alerts often include a tiny still from a surveillance video of an unidentifiable person wearing a hat.

A pair of students trip past. They're dressed in fishnet tights and boots and puffy coats.

A dark street heading west is bordered on one side by a hospital with a bad reputation, and on the other by a doomed cathedral, unfinished since 1841 and, though built of stone, prone to catching fire. The ambulances unload in its shadow, beneath the hourly striking of its bell. Email didn't exist when I was a college student; however we did have one of the earliest email-like systems. The dorms and libraries were connected by cables over which we could send messages through our computers. This brand-new technology possessed a throwback, Cold War allure. It was invented in a building that perpetually hummed like a transfer station, and had many nonaccessible subfloors on which, it was rumored, the government computer to launch the country's nuclear warheads was hidden.

An empty ambulance, lights flashing, drives away as the bell sounds. My college didn't use its communication system to send alerts about nonaffiliate-on-affiliate crime, maybe because there wasn't much of it in a small town inhabited predominantly by wealthy retirees. Neither my workplace nor my college used their systems to alert affiliates of other crime variations. Affiliate-on-affiliate crime. Affiliate-on-nonaffiliate. My two college roommates and I hosted an affiliate-on-nonaffiliate crime in our freshman dorm room one month after we arrived. The victim was a high school lacrosse recruit. My roommate took the recruit to classes, lacrosse practice, dinner, and a party. The two of them talked to a varsity hockey player. He walked them back to the dorm because the recruit was staying on our couch. After we'd gone to bed, the hockey player returned, opened the unlocked door, and raped the recruit while my two roommates and I slept on the other side of a thin partition.

Though not part of the orientation we received as new students, this sequence of events, and its outcome, became part of the unofficial one. Only once, in four years, did I forget what I'd been taught. One night, after a stressful exam period, I passed out in the upstairs bedroom of a fraternity house. The next morning, as I was headed home, a brother stopped me on the staircase. He reported that he'd seen a stranger ogling me through the bedroom door I'd failed to even close. The stranger called him over and suggested that the two of them go inside, lock the door, and have sex with me.

At first I was confused. Was the brother telling me what had happened to me while I was unconscious? That I'd been raped by two men? Then I understood. I thanked the brother for not letting the stranger rape me, and for not raping me himself. I really did feel grateful on both counts.

The brother said, *In the future, you need to be careful.*

The café near the cathedral is full of melancholic graduate students. They'd all be smoking if it were still allowed. Whenever I pass this café, I think of the mistakes I made, and the delusions I suffered. I was working at the time (I was a graduate student) on a book of flawed stories. They were so flawed that they caused me actual nausea while writing them. And yet I'd sit down each day and make them worse. Now I tout the virtues of this approach to students. Mistakes are valuable. Failure is valuable. Maybe that's true, but as a general principle, it isn't transferable, at least when there's more than one person involved, because when there is, that other person, in addition to being the teacher, must either be the victim or the perp.

Around the corner from the café is the university's very short fraternity row but it's too early yet for parties. After the recruit was raped in my dorm room, the collective shock on our floor quickly took the form of skepticism. How could this have occurred in such a small suite without my roommates and me hearing it? The walls in the dorm were so thin. They let all the sounds through. You could hear a person reading. How could a crime make no noise? How could a crime not melt the drywall tape, the spackle? Skeptics worried over acoustics and architecture. They measured the distance between our beds and the couch with their eyes. If the room's floor plan did not support what happened, then no one needed to confront the core implausibility: how the hockey player could have raped this girl.

I turn north on Broadway and head toward home. The recruit, the whispers suggested, should accept some responsibility for contributing to her rape's implausibility. The disbelief had a tinge of blame to it. Even my roommate, who'd hosted the recruit, was doubtful, though her suspicion was guilt in disguise. She felt to blame for what happened to the recruit. Everyone was blamed except the hockey player. I wasn't exactly blamed by the fraternity brother who kept me from being raped in the fraternity, but he warned me how, in the future, if I wasn't careful, I might be.

The sidewalk is empty save for a woman in a long shearling coat. She looks like she hasn't slept in days. She veers from her lane, crosses into mine, and asks for directions to the nearest subway entrance.

I'm asked for directions five days out of seven. It's not clear why. Maybe because I look every stranger in the face. I appear nice, knowledgeable, and patient. I can help. But lately, I've begun to wonder if they think they're the ones helping me.

I tell her: It's not far. The first entrance she'll pass is not an entrance, it's an exit. The entrance is another half block north. She can enter on the uptown side because both platforms can be reached. Even if she's going downtown, she doesn't have to cross the street.

Thanks, she says.

She stumbles off in the wrong direction. In trying to verbally map her every possible move and mistake, I've made her more lost, rather than less. In the future, I'll try not to think so much about the future. The future is a blame trap. It's also the place where I'm closer to death and my children are grown. Why would I want to spend all of my time there? It's late but I'm not ready to go home. To the east, I hear singing. It might be a student group performing on the library steps. I walk toward the sound. It's coming from the cathedral. Who is in the cathedral at this time of night? The doors are shut. The windows don't open. Yet the voices are piercingly clear as they pass through the stone walls, the ones that somehow catch fire.

The report is due. I've put it off and off, and now I'm cramming like the students I can see in the dorm windows across the street.

The new file glows emptily. The report must be four pages long. Colleagues submit what amounts to a term paper on the work of other colleagues when those colleagues come up for review. It's like being in high school and writing a paper on Kafka if the assignment is to prove to a Kafkaesque committee why Kafka shouldn't lose his job.

Fortunately, today, the report is about a person whose work I unconditionally love. The report must adhere to a certain form. Some claim that the form makes the task easy; the writer just fills in the blanks.

But the form makes me want to do violence to something I need, like my computer. On the other side of the wall, to the immediate left of my desk, which is in a dead-end hallway, a little girl screams. She does this every afternoon for a few hours.

Today I want to scream along with her.

I finish the opening paragraph. The exhausted mother says, during a lull in the daughter's storm, and with no judgment—like me, she's respecting a form and reporting the facts—*You are being unfriendly and unkind.*

I'm halfway through the first section, enumerating the many ways the colleague has positively influenced the field. Suddenly, the yelling to my left is accompanied by banging to my right. My husband decided he could live no longer in a zombie war zone and so moved the video console into our son's bedroom, which is ten feet from my "office," and which has effectively become his office. He has an office chair. He wears headphones with a mic and sounds like a stockbroker, at least the ones in the movies who yell in a panic, *Sell! Sell! Dump it all now!*

He's been relatively quiet this evening, but because he's either lost or won, he starts hitting his desk and saying, loudly, in a steady, unpunctuated stream, *Guys guys GUYS, I also have oh my god can you let me talk PLEASE I also have the gun for the specter, he's at three hundred, grab an angle and hold it, yeah, yeah, I know that glitch, that was embarrassing for all of us, thank you, nice one, boys, nice playing, nice.*

At least he's saying please and thank you.

One of the boys he plays with is older than he is. In school, they aren't friends. Arguably, they aren't friends online, either. I've never met this boy, but what I've heard through the door makes him sound like a bully. He used to make my son cry a lot. Now rarely. Now, having learned to survive both in the game and with his online social group, my son also sometimes sounds like a bully. He's clarified, when I cautiously express concern over what sounds like cruel jabs bordering on harassment, that he and his group are just trash-talking. It helps with performance, he claims, and is a form of casual conversation. The group recently expanded to include some boys in Nashville. What he's reported to me about these boys: One has a dead mother. One was diagnosed as a "mild" sociopath. When I asked how he learned these personal details, given what usually passes for communication between them, he said, with a shrug, *We talk.*

Now the chaos is in stereo. The girl behind the left wall, the boys behind the right.

I knock on my son's door and say, Keep it down.

Okay, he says.

I return to my desk. It's my policy never to eavesdrop, but then I hear the phrase "my mom," and so, by rights, because my name has been invoked, I'm allowed to listen. I tiptoe back to the door. The boys are discussing mothers and how theirs are always correcting them.

Even the boy with the dead mother is chiming in with complaints.

My son says, with chummy exasperation, My mom does that, too.

I return to my desk. I begin the second section of the report. Suddenly, it's a relief to have a form to fill. The colleague's teaching evaluations are pristine—on the 0–5, Poor-to-Excellent scale, they're unfailingly Excellent. The only 0 they receive is about the condition of the classroom.

The doorbell rings. The food is here.

My son's room erupts in yelling.

I knock.

What, he says, which is how he gives me permission to enter.

Though he's been told he cannot eat or drink in his room, there's an empty soda bottle under his chair and some tiny plastic oil drums on the desk half-filled with neon liquid candy. Dirty shirts and socks are scattered over the floor, as though he's been electrocuted and the voltage blew his clothing off. His room would definitely score a 0 on any evaluation form. The room's long, narrow shape is made narrower by the rows of overstuffed bookshelves running along the walls. He basically sleeps in a library annex between the stacks. The single window is half-blocked by an air conditioner that runs all winter, because the radiator's valve is broken and can't be turned off. The wastefulness of this "fix"—heating and cooling simultaneously—is part of the room's history. The space struggles to support human life and I'm honoring that struggle. My son was born in this room.

It's time to get off, I say.

Just one more minute, he says.

No, now, I say. It's dinnertime now.

If I leave the game early, he says, I'll be banned from the game.

This is what he always says. This is how I always respond.

The game is a business. The business needs you to buy skins and weapons and other things that cost nothing to produce, because they don't physically exist, and environmentally this is actually fairly responsible, save for the electricity needed to run the servers, which is why I give you money to support this business, which wouldn't survive a fortnight—ha—if it banned its customers from spending money just because they needed to eat.

During dinner, I don't mention what I overheard. I don't want him to feel eavesdropped upon or given more reason to resent, simply because there's no other place for my desk, that I'm stationed like the speech police outside his door.

I suggest, because the two of us are alone tonight, that we could watch a zombie movie. He and I have been making our way through the zombie canon. He loves scary, gory movies where displays of common humanity are punishable by death. At first the plots alone were the entertainment; now the entertainment is making fun of the plots. Zombie movies, even the best ones, rely on people behaving stupidly to maximize the body count or to drape an emotional skin over what is otherwise a first-person-shooter game. Yes, it's moving that the father, in order to save his daughter, sacrifices himself. But his sacrifice was unnecessary. He could have pushed his former friend, now a zombie, off the train. Instead, he hesitated, and got bitten, and his daughter had to watch him change into a monster and die.

Idiot, my son will say, of characters like the father. I love critiquing movies with him, but I also miss the person who found so moving the story of the boy who carried his zombie sister in a box, and who was not stupid, he was heartbreaking and committed, because he believed against all evidence: Inside the monster she was still alive.

Tonight, we choose a zombie movie that stars a family. As coincidence, or convention, would have it, the mother is a scold, jumping on her husband, an international government investigator on leave, for the slightest domestic infraction. But then he's recalled to duty because of a zombie invasion, and the family moves to an aircraft carrier. Despite the chaos, the wife remains resistantly unaware of the genre her life belongs to. She still thinks she's in a rom-com. She shushes the husband—*you'll wake up the girls*—when he whisperingly strategizes with his commander about how to save the world. While cozy in her berth, she calls her husband on a satellite phone to check in and say good night. He's sneaking past some zombies when his phone rings, and the zombies spot them, and attack them, and kill a popular soldier.

As the movie runs, I persistently mock not the wife but the stock character that is the wife. She isn't a person so much as a male screenwriter in stay-at-home-mom drag. Her "cautions" are misplaced, silly, and out of touch, even as, I point out, she's often being gaslit. Why is it her fault for calling her husband—he gave her the phone, and she doesn't know, as the husband has discovered on this mission, that zombies can't smell or see and respond only to sound—and not his fault for forgetting to turn off his ringer?

My son joins in. He makes fun of her, too, understanding, I'm pretty certain, that we're not making fun of *her*. I don't know if he suspects that I heard him speaking to his friends. I don't know if he understands that we're critiquing more than just this apocalypse.

The movie is over. The family survives. This has been fun, but he's got his own surviving to do. He returns to his room and puts on his headset. *Hey, boys, I'm back.*

I fold the laundry mounded on the couch, which my son used as a pillow during the movie. I knock and he says, What, and I put his clothes on his bureau. His desk chair is located exactly where the birth tub was. Then I shut the door and try not to listen as he talks to his friends. *Bro, how do you know you can't even hear foot-steps, no, no, do not stay up there, can you get a new angle, PLEASE.* They are maybe my opponents and, also, for the duration of the game, they are his. But even this part of his life, which multiply threatens my extinc-tion, isn't without its touching moments that differently break my heart. If he's old enough to start missing things other than me, I'm also losing him to loss. *Boys, remem-ber how much we used the pink in the beginning. That was our only skin.*

Something's been eating a coat in the barn. I shouldn't keep coats out there because they get mildewed, but this coat, when I bought it, had insects living in the fur, and so I thought I'd freeze them to death over the winter. But now a different creature has found it. Probably one of the mice or porcupines or raccoons. The skunks recently made their nest under my office, now its own ecosystem. Wasps and birds in the eaves. Squirrels in the walls. Skunks under the floorboards, rustling around, and emitting a faint gasoline odor through the cracks.

The coat's half-eaten hood hangs off the shoulders like a chunky fur net.

Clearly, it's time again to straighten the barn and re-

mind everyone of their boundaries. Where we are allowed to go. Where the animals are. I have much more
time to clean these days. When it's my turn to watch my
son, I'm not technically watching anyone. I'm just the
designated person on call, should he need money or
food, or medical assistance, or a ride.

The kitchen door slams. I hear boys run through the
house, and out the back, and then the jalopy groan of
the trampoline. My daughter is sunbathing on a towel
nearby, listening to music on her phone. She tends to
ignore her brother unless there's some drama with his
friends.

Right now, one of my son's friends is teasing him. Between the squeaking of the springs, I hear the friend announce to my daughter, who's apparently shown enough
interest to remove an earbud: He and my son were at
the general store this morning. A woman stopped them
out front.

She told your brother, *You will grow up to be a very
beautiful woman,* his friend says, laughing.

I hear my son gripe about being mistaken for a girl,
not once, but three times today.

My daughter says something that I cannot hear.

I move the broken chairs to a different corner and
dust the tool bench. Beneath is a basket of toys—a doll-
size cast-iron stove, a set of doll-size wooden cups and
plates. In addition to books, I also bought toys for my
children before they were born. I couldn't wait to play
with these toys and assumed any child of mine, if I had

one, would feel the same. Neither of them ever once played with the stove or the plates. Yet I can't give them away. They make me miss something that's forever gone and never existed in the first place. I should have let my friend's daughter take them. When this friend came to visit, I took out the basket, and her daughter unpacked everything with obsessive care. She cooked on the stove and set a table for tiny, pretend animals, even though there were plenty of real ones nearby. The little girl became so sad when her mother said it was time to go, and she had to put the stove and plates away. I almost said, Just take them! But I didn't. When I thought of the little girl walking away, holding the toys my children never played with, I couldn't breathe.

I take all the objects out of the drawers of the bench. A darning egg. A packet of spare wicks. A rusted tin pan.

Beneath it is the collection of Annunciation postcards, wrapped in a hair scrunchie.

The postcards are wavy now, and brittle, shedding a sawdust-like powder. They're core samples recording the barn's weather. Freezes followed by damp thaws by dry heat by damp cool by freezes. I'm mad at myself for forgetting that there's no benign neglect in this house, anything left in a drawer or a box will be ruined, because damage comes to things unused. The baby clothes I kept in the storage space, the mice found them, and shat and peed all over them, though it was hard to think they'd mistreated the tiny pants and onesies, because they'd been shat and peed on by my children. The mice had a point, one my husband shares, about my inability to get rid of the clothing, as if my children might ever fit in them again. They shat and peed on that delusion. They forced me to throw the stinking bag away.

There's no one to play this game with and so I play it with myself.

Mary. Flip. Mary. Flip.

Back in the house, there's an unusual sound. The house has been making a lot of them lately, moaning for attention. Last week, the basement flooded. The sump pump, for whatever reason, wasn't working again. It fails so regularly that I've come to think of it like the engine on *Second Chance*, a thing that exists only so that it can be fixed. To rely on it is to need many more chances than two.

From the top of the stairs, the basement resembles a lake. Even the dirty plastic tarp that covers the ground, and presents moisture from further rotting the joists, is submerged. I put on rubber boots and wade through the water to the corner where the sump pump chugs futilely. The hose, when I feel it, is full of air. I shake it, and reposition it, and finally whatever was blocking the hose jogs loose. The water levels fall and the plastic resurfaces. Puddles form in the thick wrinkles like tidal pools on a rock. It sometimes feels safest in this basement because it's freest from delusion. Upstairs, the plaster can be spackled, the paint refreshed. Down here the machines panic and fail. The water rises beneath the leggy shadows of the abandoned fuel tanks. The house is little different from a boat, or a well, or a grave. What I find most touching is how beautiful the stone foundation walls are, the ones that keep the dirt sides from collapsing and with them the entire house. They will forever keep this hole from becoming the remains of one. Someone put an incredible amount of time into building these walls, yet who would ever see them? They're soothing to look at, and so possibly were built not only to keep the hole a hole, but to also send calming messages to whoever was crouching in the mud. *Some things never fail.* When a mason came to build a stone retaining wall by the kitchen, he let me place an actual message into the center of it when he was half finished. I found the sturdiest ziplock bag. I wrote the note in pencil, not pen, in case the bag leaked, and the paper got wet, and the ink ran. I wanted it to be legible for hundreds and hundreds of years, to reassure whoever came after us that the trouble was worth it, and to never tear the house down. *Here lived a happy family*, I wrote. Then I worried that this message would be differently illegible hundreds of years from now. What is a family? Would the word or the concept even exist? But as the mason sealed the bag into the wall, I realized the utter futility of the note, no matter what it said, because the circumstances allowing a person to find it would imply: The house was already gone.

The sun beats through the windows. It's still morning but already so hot.

My son is awake and banging on his desk.

There's no way, I say to his door, that you're staying inside all day to yell at your friends through a headset.

I pack food and towels and a football and try not to ask questions that are poorly disguised criticisms. *What child does not want to go to the beach?*

Once on the highway, he asks how long it will take to get there.

I lie and say, Not long.

I try to brighten the vibe in the car by asking about the flag football game he played yesterday. I might siphon some joy from the past into the present because his team won on the final play, but he just wants to gripe about the officiating. The ref refused to give him a first down during a play when he broke free of the defenders and ran the length of the field.

The reason the run didn't count, I say, was because a teammate was called for blocking.

He doesn't believe me.

I was on the sidelines, I say. I heard the coach ask the ref about the call, and the ref said, *blocking*.

No, he says. I got the first down.

If a player ran the length of the field, I say, the only reason, absent a penalty, they wouldn't get a first down, is if the ref had never played or watched football in his entire life.

But that's what *happened*, he says.

He's determined to believe he was uniquely wronged by the ref, as, I now understand, I've uniquely wronged him by making him go to the beach.

The road is paved with trucks belching yellow exhaust. The online map reroutes us over a different bridge, and coincidentally, he also switches directions. He admits that he was confused. We were talking about different plays.

We are both wrong and both right.

A causeway leads to a rotary circling a monument that looks like a crematorium. It's hard to discern which beach is the right beach, because the friends we're meeting gave directions based on recollections they admitted were vague. *You'll see numbered parking fields on the*

*left, but do not park there, keep driving until you see
fields on the beach side, but do not park in the first field
you see, park in the second or the third field, the number
might be either 4 or 9.*

I park in Field 6, and unload the bags, and walk
toward the water and shake out the blanket.

My son pulls off his shirt. He is so tall, suddenly. That
person I caught a quick glimpse of, all those years ago,
sprinting around the house in rain boots, he is now him.

My friends arrive. Their son runs to join mine, bob-
bing just beyond the break. He's younger and smaller.
He hesitates at the foamy lip. My son stays farther out.
The current is strong and pulls him sideways. I have to
constantly check his location. After an hour, I walk to
the water and beg him to rest, by which I mean *I* need a
rest from tracking him. Finally, he drags himself to
shore like a shipwreck survivor. He heaves himself onto
a blanket and takes a brief nap. Then the group goes for
a walk. My son and the younger boy find a tidal pool
and a stick and dig a trench to the waves.

I also find a stick. Everyone is busy working. Nobody
talks and the gulls are loud. Overhead, a plane drags a
banner that asks, *Do You Love Saving Money?* But all I
see, as the banner flutters and grows smaller and increasingly hard to read, is *Do You Love.*

By the time we return to the blanket, our food has
been stolen by a gull. The wind is strong and the temperature drops. I pack up the blanket. My heart is as
heavy as the bag, which contains a lot of seawater, dis-

persed among the towels. Before getting in the car, my
son changes out of his bathing suit, which has an aston-
ishing amount of sand in it, like maybe five pounds'
worth. How had he managed to stay afloat with so much
extra weight?

He discovers a hot soda under his seat. His mood is
brighter than it's been in days. He's tired and sunburned
and his face is as available to me again as if he were six.
I push my nose against his nose and look into his eyes
and say, Have I ever steered you wrong, or made you do
something that was not fun? Can you admit that I have
good ideas, and that I will always lead you to the waves?

I can still spot, in the darkest recesses of his pupils,
the microsecond of fear that flashes when I ask him a
question, and he understands it as a test or a scold—*why
does he put small objects in his mouth*—or feels pressure
to give the right answer, because he wants to make me
happy. But the flash is so weak. It's barely discernible
and might not have existed at all. It might have been the
sun, reflecting off the side mirrors of the cars still in the
lot.

I don't need you to answer those questions, I say.

I hold his face and hope that he can hear me, even
though I'm no longer speaking: I understand the joys of
being unknown, and unfindable, to people who love you.
That time I left my phone below the tide line, I didn't
replace it for five months. One night, I drove around
alone, and visited one friend, and then another and then
another, and none of the people at home who loved me

most, and whom I loved most, knew where I was, and not that I was trying to escape them, but the freedom I felt, that night, when my location was a secret, I understand why he'd want to feel that freedom, too.

I kiss him and give him a pillow so he can nap on the ride back. I pull up the phone map and select our destination: home.

Instead of sleeping, he stares out the window. I can sense, as though it's accompanied by a noise or a smell, his consciousness exiting the car and commingling with the blur beyond the car windows. I remember how gloriously big I could feel as a small child, how bursting and arcing toward a future self, when trapped in a seat and speeding through space under the care of a person I trusted and loved, and to whom I less and less exposed my interior, at least not in words.

The low sun burns through the faraway city. The day feels charged. Poles flipping. Stars replaced by other stars. The reliable bodies once used to locate myself, and others in relation to me, are shifting and weakening. For him, I am no longer his sole point of orientation and will never be again. He will not always be mine. This is the most disorienting. The dispersing of the intensity of my love, by which I mean the heart-hurting, hourly need, for first my daughter, and then my son, feels like homesickness for homesickness. It's similar to the pull I feel when driving over the failing bridge, looking toward the islands and harbors I visited with my family. My childhood, and theirs, are both behind me, visible only from a great height, and impossible to touch. I've been grieving this moment for years in advance, reduced myself, at times, to head-holding, breathless despair. It's over, it's over, it's over. This is true. But Polaris, for reasons nobody understands, has been getting brighter as Earth's axis slowly tilts away from it. The relationship of inconsequence to clarity is inverted where stars, and maybe humans, too, are concerned.

The car comes to a stop in the middle of the highway. The brake lights sketch a red line between the trees. The future is stillness. The present is stillness. My phone suggests a faster route home, but heartbreak is the only compass. It says to stay the course and make this moment last.

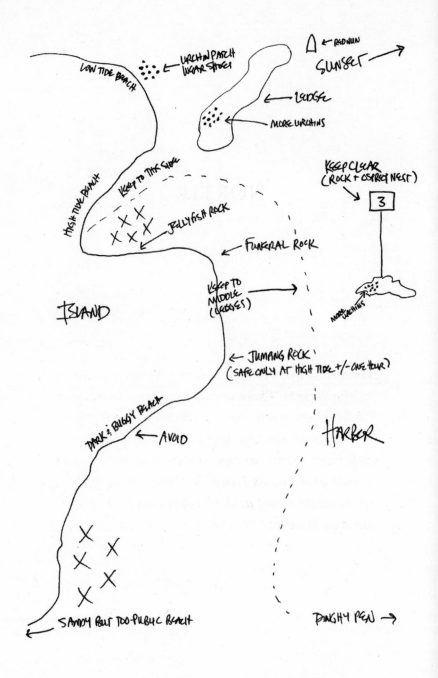

NORTH

When it is thick or rough down the bay, retreat to the Reach. There are snug and attractive harbors on each end. Dangers are clearly marked and easily avoided. The tide does not run hard except at the east end between the Castle and Devils Head. It floods in at both ends, meets about at the bridge, and flows out the way it came.

I wake up at 3 AM, just as I did with my daughter. This is the Witching Hour, when the veil between the living and the dead is rumored to be the thinnest. Labor can feel like a haunting because it can lead to death, sometimes more than one. People have been dying in childbirth for a thousand years and labor unites us. With my daughter, during the twenty-seven hours we lived between worlds, I felt more connected, as the pain swelled and ebbed, withdrew and revisited, to this lineage of strangers than I did to the human inside me that I hoped would choose life, and let me keep mine.

This time, however, I can't as easily slip between worlds. I have attachments. I get into my daughter's bed and hold her and say good-bye. I say it over and over into her sleeping body. I'm more confident, this time, that I'll survive the trip. But she will never again be the only person with whom I've traveled through in-between places. And I'll be bringing someone back.

I walk north to the dark living room and get on my knees to plug in the tree. Some say the Witching Hour corresponds with the time that Jesus died on the cross. Jesus was also born on this day, not that we're celebrating him. We're just in it for the presents. But as the pain increases, what might seem an irony, or a cruel reminder of what existence boils down to, minus the life—a birthday and a crucifixion—will instead, for the indefinite future, be the only way to perceive.

When the sun rises, it's time for everyone to get out of the apartment. Whereas last night I could not stop hugging my daughter, now I need her to leave me. My husband packs her a bag to take to his parents' apartment, fifty blocks downtown. Her aunt and uncle and cousins are also, conveniently, there. Despite my love of planning, none of this has been planned. All is luck. This is happening two weeks earlier than predicted.

For the last time, our family of three takes the elevator to the lobby. I make a very small deal of that moment when, on the street, they head north toward the train, and I walk west, toward the park.

The entrance is at the top of the sledding hill. Here, people take chances with children they otherwise overprotect, shoving them toward benches and trees, nominally buffered by hay bales that rarely survive past the first snow, after which they're removed by the college students and repurposed for jumps. I often marvel at these parents' sudden, giddy flip, as if they've been struck on the head themselves, and, venting from the skull crack all that's so worried and driven them, are finally able to release themselves and their children to the wilds of chance. These children whose bodies were the closely monitored repositories of supposed virtue, their parents suddenly relinquish to the air and watch them fly away.

But today there's no snow. The hill is vacant and scraped down to mud. Along the promenade, lone people sit on benches. Christmas may be one of the more famous birthdays, but it's also a day when people kill themselves. I try not to look any of them in the eye. None of us want to be seen right now. We are animals needing solitude, which in a city is hard to find. There are not enough bushes, not enough silence, at best there's wind and a woody clatter of trash, and sometimes a damp, fecal stench near the stone retaining wall, inside of which the raccoons live.

After a mile, I turn back toward home, and climb the stairs to the apartment, and discuss with my husband, who has returned without our daughter, whether or not it's time to call the midwife. I chose this midwife because her cold gruffness signaled that she'd be good in a crisis, but something prevents me, when I presumably need her most, from dialing her number. Only now is it apparent: She is the wrong person for this job. I should have chosen a midwife like the one I had for my daughter's birth, who called each contraction like she was a hushed commentator at a sporting event where the athletes needed silence to concentrate, and whose mother named her after someone she met in a dream.

Finally, my husband and I decide: It's time. Another Witching Hour in a day of witching has passed. Each completed orbit on this clock thins and thins the membrane covering the abyss where the self is annihilated and becomes the ghostly bridge connecting life with life. But the midwife doesn't pick up. I leave her a message. *Just checking in and hope you're having a great day*, I say, as if she were my client, and not the reverse.

Thirty minutes later, when she calls back, she's at a spa across state lines. She makes self-evident observations like *I guess you're having a baby*, which in addition to being self-evident, sounds like she's disappointed, as though all these months she believed I'd be different from her other clients, but apparently I'm not. For my failure to be other than what I am, therefore making her none other than what she is, she's in no hurry to get in her car.

My husband and I try to watch a movie. Then we take another walk. The winter sun makes the day feel even colder and emptier. The calm should be soothing but it's not. Absent all the harried people with goals to absorb the light, every facet glints. The buildings flash too many messages and my eyes register the air as *so loud*. We retreat to the apartment, but the lowering sun reflects off the dorm across the street, and the windows bounce the light into our home, and the world seems twisted on its axis, the sunset flaring to the east.

I call the midwife again and ask her to come. While we wait for her to cross the bridge that spans the river, my husband calls his sister. She tells him all we've missed: who opened what and what was hidden inside which-size box.

When the midwife arrives, she feels around and gives her verdict. Very little to report. She spreads paperwork on the dining room table and starts to pay bills. It's hard not to take her scribbling and tearing and licking personally, as though she's implying that having failed to not have a baby, I am now having a baby but failing. Then she gets a phone call from her backup midwife. Another client, with whom it seems I am in competition for her services, has a lot to report. The midwife is suddenly like a person wanting to go to a better party, and this seems like an excellent opportunity for everyone to get what they want.

I urge her to go, and say, *Good luck!* as if I'll never see her again.

Things quickly get worse, or better, depending on the desired outcome: a lot of pain with an end, or some pain with no end.

I encourage my husband to try to sleep, because one of us needs to be rested. I walk east, and then south along the windows, and then west through the kitchen, and then north toward the dining room. I repeat this loop 800 billion times. I feel lonely and then special and then lonely and then really lonely, like I'm a person on a park bench suspended for eternity in darkness without a knife to cut my throat.

On one of the many loops, I consider—as I often do, and as I've encouraged my daughter to do—the emotional state of the professor who lives on the other side of the west wall. She's been diagnosed with ALS and her every conscious moment could be described as suspended for eternity in darkness without a knife. When my daughter throws tantrums, I tell her to have sympathy for the woman because she cannot escape the noise, she is trapped in her body in her bed in her apartment. Now, however, I'm the one making the noise that the woman cannot escape. On my face, which no one can see, I show no fear. I show no emotion. If my face knows it, I will know it. If my face is blank, so am I. I keep walking. I will never stop. Dining room–hallway–kitchen–hallway. Table–chair–stove–books. I wonder: In what direction does time move? When I'm in labor, time travels in an east–west circle. It spirals and tightens. Otherwise, time is liquid silver and hard to catch. I have to chase it as it travels north.

Finally, I wake my dozing husband. Having few midwifery skills, his job is to make me laugh, and to mock the situation in which we find ourselves, as a way of lessening its power to terrify us both. He's yet to read the book about how to be a good birth partner, and so he skims it in a velvet armchair while I crouch on the bed. This book, we discover together, seems primarily interested in reassuring the birth partner that their experience is equally valid. At the end of the chapter is a section called "What You Might Be Feeling."

He asks me, from the velvet, between pain strikes: Do you want to know what *I'm* feeling?

We laugh until the pauses separating one clench from the next are so minuscule that there's no time to do anything inside of them but breathe. He stays very calm, and calls the midwife, who sounds atypically energized and sparkly. She's not even on speaker and I can hear her from the other room. The other client has just given birth and everyone's goofy with endorphins. She's about to weigh the baby on that scale she showed me during one of our meetings, a tiny cloth hammock attached to a hook.

After which, she says, she'll jump right in her car.

But things are moving quickly. Faster than the midwife. My first midwife, the one named after a person in her mother's dream, takes over. She sportscasts from my brain. The game clock is ticking down. It's the fourth quarter, fifth set, ninth inning, no overtime. My husband calls the midwife again, increasingly nervous. She stays on speakerphone, reporting her progress as she drives. She is on Thirty-ninth street. She is on Fifty-sixth. Eighty-seventh. One hundred and tenth. Her progress is ticks on a ruler. My progress is measurable in depths. As a child, it felt so scary when, on the boat with my family, the depth sounder measured feet beneath our hull greater than a hundred. Would Earth still hold us to it? Or would gravity be so weakened that we'd spin like I'm spinning now, my body a room without boundaries, so I'm loose and crashing around inside it? Sounding is distance and distance both noise and lack of noise. The less noise, the farther from the ocean floor, and so, while on a boat, a person wants silence, total silence. Inside I'm nothing but noise, yet why can't I see the bottom?

The midwife arrives. Her job concludes at the moment it begins. Out comes the rope that my husband cuts and everyone is free. We eat the lemon tart he made for the holiday dinner we didn't attend. I think again of the neighbor in the next-door apartment. We sort of spent the holiday together. I hoped the sounds I made helped her feel less alone. Within earshot, another person was trapped inside a body, and there was no way out save through.

The midwife leaves. My son sleeps against my side, millimeters away from a place he just left forever.

We travel north, north, north, north, north, north, north, north, north.

When my son is ten, he asks about the night he was born. He rarely asks, anymore, to hear true stories about my life, though technically this isn't about my life, it's the very first story about his. I tell him how what I remember most vividly was the path we both took. I walked for longer than a day; I traveled a measurable distance through time and space to give birth to him.

Somehow, this description doesn't satisfy him, or even capture his interest.

But I've been prepared for this day. In the trunk of the car is a very long piece of orange rope.

The day is warm, and the tide is coming.

We drive to the boatyard and climb into the dinghy. My son knows how to row but pretends he can't. At camp, he rows and canoes and paddles and sails. When he refuses to take the oars, he's drawing a line and saying: *Here is my life. Here is yours.*

I suggest we go to the island that forms the harbor. I take every opportunity, as we thread our way between the boats and past the giant metal barge that sets moorings, the bow of which is seamed by a heavy chain that lifts and lowers many hundred-pound concrete blocks, to give survival tips. I show him how to tell if there's a current, and where it's coming from, by looking at the lobster buoys, to see if the water forms, as it flows around them, a rippled V. Knowing the tide and also the wind direction is important. He must be mindful of the trickiness of sandbars. A land bridge between islands can, within minutes, become submerged. I tell him about the deaths that have occurred on those bars, people swept away by a tide pulling out or in. I warn him how, in the narrowest spots between islands, when the tide is at its strongest, it will be impossible to fight against it.

He doesn't appear to be listening, but this is how he

listens. All of these words are dropped like blocks of concrete to his ocean floor, to hopefully tether whatever
thoughts or actions might someday float on his surface.

Because the tide is almost high, there's an accessible
beach on the southwestern end of the island. When the
tide is low, it's impossible to reach or even see this beach,
disguised behind a sloped fortress of rocks. For three
quarters of the tide cycle, the shore is chunked up and
slimed. But for one quarter, it resembles white, powdery
Greece. It's also undeniable now—the island is sick. Or
rather, its trees are. A virus has started to kill them off.
Soon this windbreak between the harbor and the ocean
will no longer exist. The harbor will no longer be one.

We pass *Vixen, Dolphin, Sheila-Marie*. The other
boats that formed the code we wrote a few years back
are gone. The owners died and the boats were sold.
They're in some other harbor now and might return
only if they've struck a ledge and need fixing.

We pass the rock where people jump at high tide. It's
shaped like a planet. You have to run from the edge of
the trees and feel with your feet where the curved surface turns too steeply vertical, and push off before the
slope sucks you down, and into the water just beneath
the rock, where a ledge fans out, covered in barnacles.
We've analyzed the rock at different tides. We know the
best approach, angle, technique. This also counts as a
survival lesson. Here I'm like those parents on the sledding hill. I let my children fly.

We pass the rock where my funeral will be. It slopes

more gradually into the water, like the flank of a whale. It faces northwest toward the failing bridge. The sunset is webbed by its cables, the faint, black lines stabilizing the flames. I've given very specific directions to my children about how my funeral should run. They've been instructed to stand on this rock at around 6 PM in early August. The tide should be high, and the wind blowing not at all or from the south, so that the rock will be in the lee. First they should go for a swim. Maybe out around the nearest boat and back, because the water temperature won't be terrible at that time of year, 58 degrees or, depending on what decade it is, considerably more. And then, while wet, and wrapped in towels, they should throw my ashes into the ocean where their bodies were just floating, supported by the chilly brine, and drink a bottle of champagne as the salt water evaporates from their skin, leaving it tight, as though every inch of them is being hugged.

I remind my son, as we pass the rock, of my wishes. He rolls his eyes and I'm glad. Everything is going to plan. I can't insist that my children tell laughingly critical stories about me at my funeral, so I must, while alive, behave in a laughable manner to have any shot of getting what I want when I'm dead. We float above the rocks, which are five feet below us, but appear much closer. Depth is deceptive. The ocean can magically swallow an oar, jabbed straight down to check how far away the bottom is. The hull makes a shushing sound as we glide over seaweed, attached to the rocks and lifted, by the water, to the surface. I pull the boat onto the beach, higher than the tide line, which is clearly marked by dead seaweed, rolled tight like a long, skinny cigar and home to a billion sand fleas, the ones shaped like minuscule shrimp. I remind my son not to kick the seaweed or the fleas will be released. I remind him that he must not leave a boat below that line if the tide is coming, or the boat will float away.

I show him how to tie a knot in the painter and loop it around a rock to doubly secure the boat to the land.

Now we are safe. Shipshape. It's just the two of us, plus an osprey, who swoops around a nest on top of a sick tree. Tiny heads cheep in the splintery shag. The osprey carves increasingly wider circles, coming nearer and nearer to us, trying to ascertain if we're danger.

I don't think that we are, but I don't know what counts as danger to this bird. I can't guess the threat I might represent, what present or future damage I might inflict. I'm eroding this beach, distressing those fleas. I'm raising and releasing this boy.

My son is by the rocks where once we found a jellyfish. We put it inside a jar, and then we buried it, and dug it up later, and the stink was so awesome it felt like the universe had torn open and we were experiencing life, pure life.

He says, Remember the time we put the dead jellyfish in the jar?

I do. He stands beside me. The top of his head is nearly at my chin. On this beach, holding this rope, I don't know that, by the time he's eleven, he'll hit his growth spurt. He'll grow six inches in a year, and then keep growing, and no matter how many new pants my husband buys for him, they are always, within weeks, ending above his ankles again. He'll become nearer to an adult while his friends are still children, and I will feel robbed. His body stole two years from me. Soon I'll no longer remember, physically remember, what it was like to lie in his bed and hold his hand while he fell asleep.

I think perhaps I know this. He'll be gone sooner than most. He's on a quicker path, and this is why it's essential that he learn certain skills. How not to be stranded; how not to disturb. How to measure fathoms with a rope, in case the electronics fail. How to know if he's too far from the earth, or too close.

I stretch the rope between our hands and count my way across the beach. When he asks how long a fathom is, I don't want to say. The answer is six feet, but we are not dealing with the quantifiable. Fathoms are the stuff of stories. I want to preserve within the measurement of a fathom its unfathomableness. This is what I want to convey. His growing up is unfathomable to me, even as I can precisely mark the distance.

My son is two fathoms away. He is three fathoms. He is four, seven, ten.

As the tide rises and the beach shrinks, I start to lay the rope on the sand. I re-create the path the two of us took together before his cord was cut and our individual expeditions began. But my son is no longer watching. He's skipping stones near the jellyfish rock. I'm alone on this journey, surveilled only by the osprey. It circles, more calmly now, sensing my inability to cause much harm beyond making marks on the sand that the ocean will erase. I move around slowly, bent at the waist. The coils pile up. There's topography now, shadow and perspective, high points and low. In order to build up, there must be a burying. The tide creeps higher and the sky flares behind the bridge. I spiral and spiral until my hand is empty. Then it's time to go. I use my forearm as a spindle and whip the rope under my elbow and over my palm, then cinch the bundle in the middle and lock the bitter end. My son helps me shove the dinghy back into the water. As we float past the funeral rock, nothing grabs us from below. He sits in the stern, his hand directing me past boats with names we'll eventually forget. Behind him, the puffy clouds ignite. They reflect in the water. The most heart-stopping twilights are the weathery ones. The clouds become islands, released from the horizon. They swell with purple shadows and stay ablaze long after the sun is already gone.

I tell him what's behind him. I tell him what he's missing.

You have to look *now*, I say. Every second counts.

He turns around to please me, but only for a moment. He knows what kind of sunset this is. The sky will be most otherworldly right before nightfall. What's better still lies ahead. I balance out the oars and begin to row while he centers himself in the stern and holds up his hand. Left. Right. Left. Left. Boat rigging chimes from all sides. The islands are beside and below and above us. We're calm and focused. We each know our jobs. He guides us forward, to where we're going, while I keep track of what we're leaving, and where we've been.

ABOUT THE AUTHOR

HEIDI JULAVITS is the author of *The Folded Clock: A Diary* and four novels, including the PEN Award–winning *The Vanishers*. A founding editor of the literary magazine *The Believer*, she is an associate professor at Columbia University and the recipient of a Guggenheim Fellowship.

ABOUT THE TYPE

This book was set in Walbaum, a typeface designed in 1810 by German punch cutter J. E. (Justus Erich) Walbaum (1768–1839). Walbaum's type is more French than German in appearance. Like Bodoni, it is a classical typeface, yet its openness and slight irregularities give it a human, romantic quality.